PREVENTIVE CARE

PREVENTIVE CARE

Easy Exercise Against Aging

by Alice Hornbaker

with a foreword by Hans Kraus, M.D., P.C.

DRAKE PUBLISHERS INC.   New York

Published in 1974 by
Drake Publishers Inc.
381 Park Avenue South
New York, New York 10016

Library of Congress Cataloging in Publication Data

Hornbaker, Alice.
    Preventive Care; insurance against aging.

    1. Aged—Care and hygiene. I. Title.
RC952.H67   613'.04'38   74-6133
ISBN 0-87749-666-8

Printed in the United States of America

Dedication

This book is dedicated to my late parents, Ida and Al, who gave me the gift of laughter, and my first type-writer; to my three children, Chris, Holly, and Joey, who gave me their devotion while I worked; and to my husband, Joe, who gave me his love to make it all worthwhile.

Contents

Before You Read This Book

PERHAPS THE ONLY way we will ever be able to stampede people into daily exercise as part of their way of life is to suggest that it's somewhat naughty, self-indulgent, or fattening—all of which inducements seem to titillate us into doing that very thing we shouldn't. To suggest merely that something is good for you often marks it with the so-called kiss of death. To imply instead that it might make you feel sexy, wicked, or sinfully pampered usually is enticement enough.

If that is what it takes to make you incorporate Preventive Care into your everyday living pattern, I can indeed promise you all of those things. Give Preventive Care a "ninety-day-free-home-trial." You can always ask for a refund on your slim, trim, and vibrant self for the corpulent, flaccid, aging body you traded in. It's a safe guarantee, for I'll bet you will never want it back.

Alice Hornbaker

RATIONALE FOR PREVENTIVE CARE

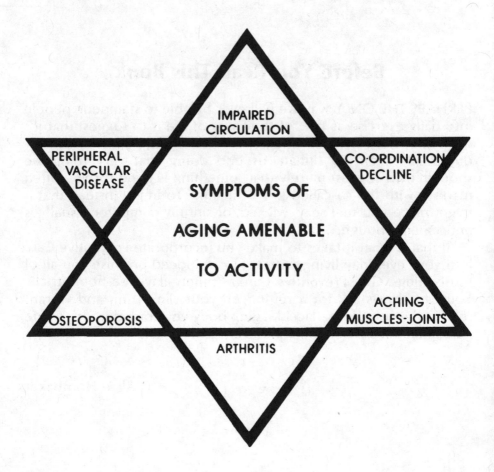

IMPAIRED
CIRCULATION

PERIPHERAL
VASCULAR
DISEASE

CO-ORDINATION
DECLINE

SYMPTOMS OF

AGING AMENABLE

TO ACTIVITY

OSTEOPOROSIS

ACHING
MUSCLES-JOINTS

ARTHRITIS

There are six symptoms of aging everyone can readily identify. But take heart. Should you find you have all six, there still is hope. The answer is to start now with low mobility exercise—Preventive Care.

Introduction

by Hans Kraus, M.D., P.C.

Associate Professor, New York University Medical School, Emeritus. Internationally known expert on back ailments and John F. Kennedy's specialist for three years. He is the author of: *Backache, Stress and Tension* (Simon & Schuster, 1965) and *Clinical Treatment of Back and Neck Pain* (McGraw-Hill, 1970).

FOR YEARS OUR experts have been debating how important physical fitness might be to maintain and restore healthful living. Abroad, with less discussion, many institutes have sprung up where under-exercised and over-stressed workers—both blue- and white-collar workers—can spend several weeks in order to be reconditioned. They are placed on a gradually increasing regimen of exercise, given an adequate diet, and housed in pleasant surroundings free of most irritations and stimuli. After a month's stay they return to work not only refreshed but well. The absenteeism rate has dropped to half of what it was in a similar period of time during which no physical reconditioning was offered.

In this country, Lawrence Frankel has struck out on his own and established an institute where he has actually accomplished, in many instances, what has been written about by so many others. Many patients can thank him for increased ability to function, to be active, and to lead an independent life. Prior to going through his reconditioning institute, they were disabled or even handicapped.

Mr. Frankel, through Alice Hornbaker, now is relating his experiences and his knowledge in this book, and rightly so, because

11

his type of prevention is still neglected. There is urgent national need for it, and I hope that his work will inspire action on a major scale.

Physical fitness for one hour daily in all schools, beginning at the first grade and continuing through all of the school years, would be the best prevention for many of the chronic degenerative ailments that plague our society. Unfortunately, this still remains a wish.

As long as we permit our population to gradually deteriorate under the influence of a sedentary and over-stimulated way of life, reconditioning places such as the one Lawrence Frankel has originated, are invaluable. They will remain invaluable even if we reach the optimum stage whereby our youth is set out on the right way of preventive exercise and a more physically active life-style.

It is my sincere hope that this book will get the attention it deserves and that it may stimulate many more centers such as Lawrence Frankel's, so fruitful under his guidance.

Preface

NO SOONER HAD I put both feet into the main lobby from the entry hall than I inhaled its acrid odor. Attempts to whitewash it with disinfectants had made it even worse. It smelled of human decay. I felt nauseous. To my sister, who accompanied me this day to visit our mother, I blurted out, "This nursing home was supposed to be different from all those others. They promised us it would be."

"Shh," she said to me. "Let's wait and see."

I looked again at the huge living room that mocked its name. There was no one living there. The plush wall-to-wall carpeting, the resplendent draperies, the period furniture, looked for all of their elegance like a setting inside a museum. There were no signs that real people lived there.

We hurried down the long corridor to the room where my mother was a patient. After her stroke she could no longer speak; her left arm and leg were useless. The doctor said there was brain damage. She was incontinent, needed twenty-four hour care. This home was to provide that.

Involuntarily I shrieked when I saw her. There, lying in that soiled bed, was a wretched human being. Her eyes bulged out in pain. Both of her arms and her legs were tied to the bedposts with strips of cloth.

My sister and I rushed to her side, untied her bonds. I punched the buzzer to summon hospital help.

"Why?" was all I could get out.

The young aide, an unskilled part-time teen-ager, was indifferent to our anger.

"Listen. We had to. She required too much attention. She was always pushing that buzzer with that good arm. Always wanted help."

"My God, then help her!"

"Hey, listen, lady, we don't have that kind of time around here. We can't be in all these rooms every minute. She's no different than the rest of these creeps . . . ."

"Creeps! I . . . ." She ran from the room before my anger exploded.

That aide was talking about *my* mother. She called her and the rest of these old people creeps. *My Mother. Our Mother.* The matriarch of our family, its brains, its beauty, its kindness. The one strong tie that bound us all together so tightly.

It was she who had taught her three daughters ("Thank God I had no boys for the Government to use for gun fodder") how to laugh during the bad times of the Depression, relish the good times, and have enough common sense to know neither condition was permanent. It was she who had before her marriage mothered a family of ten when her mother died prematurely. It was she who always stopped our budget-minded father dead, when he'd protest a new dress or special extravagance for his daughters, with her, "Let them be. They're only young once."

How prophetic of her. Young only once but old for a very long time. And, if invalid, for what seemed infinity.

As fast as we could, we dressed her. Neither of us could stop the tears—we were outraged.

We took Mother away from that nursing home and tried caring for her again in her own apartment with around-the-clock nurses. But it grew unsafe. She lit cigarettes and let them drop, starting small fires. She neither knew or understood us. Reluctantly we took her doctor's advice and found still another convalescent-nursing home where they pretended they'd provide physical therapy. Other patients told us it never happened.

My sisters and I, and our aging dad, came by to visit our dethroned matriarch. We talked to her and pushed her in a wheelchair, always hoping some miracle would tear away the veil that had dropped down over her mind and shut us out. But it never happened. It was too late for Mother.

After she died I made a vocal and written statement to *my* family that I was never to be committed to a nursing home. I wrote a "living will" to each of my children and my husband that stated I didn't want to live past the time when I could no longer think or act for myself. They were instructed to let me die.

But I don't think such a will is necessary—now. I no longer believe old age has to end as Mother's did. One man, Lawrence Frankel of Charleston, West Virginia, convinced me that this is so. He has a new concept he calls Preventive Care, which, through prescribed exercises, keeps old people in maximum health, and allows them to "reach their full potential."

Yes, potential. For within each of us there is untapped strength and mobility to maintain ourselves in good health, mental and physical, for all the days of our lives. But we have to adopt it as a life-style, not as a chore.

Many of Charleston's elderly already have. When Preventive Care began there in 1970, it set off a revolution against atrophied bones and second-class citizenship for old people. Frankel was breaking the "conspiracy of silence" the country had evoked against its elderly. It was the seniors' Emancipation Proclamation. It meant their independence.

What will Preventive Care do? Decelerate aging. Make getting old quality, not just quantity.

I invite you now, you of all ages, to read this book and join the Preventive Care Revolution against aging. It is not a medical guide. It is not a technical book. It is about love, and caring—first, love for yourself, and then, because you feel so good, love and concern for all others.

Recruit your kids, your parents, your grandparents, yourselves. Make them all aware that exercises—planned, approved, individualized exercise—can help us all. *Now.*

Preventive Care means a new life style, a new Independence Day.

Alice Hornbaker
June 1, 1974

Acknowledgments

ALL PHOTOGRAPHS IN this book were taken by William Tiernan, photographer for the *Charleston Daily Mail*.

My thanks go to the following who have helped in the production of this book: Kirk Polking, H. Joseph Chadwick, Charles Connor, William Tiernan, West Virginia's Commission on Aging, Betty Richard, Beulah Phillips, Jean Paiva, Mary Jo Foster, the Kanawha Medical Society.

Members of the Board of Directors of Frankel Foundation: Guy Erwin, president; Bill W. Backus, treasurer; Harry Henshaw, secretary; Paul Jefferson, Belford Roberts, William Thayer, Father Joseph Gillian, Hugh Davis, Philip G. Terrie, John Kelly, Mrs. Beverly Robinson, Mrs. John D. Rockefeller IV, Mrs. Samuel J. Richard, Jr., trustees; Doctors William Rossman, Thomas G. Potterfill, Carl Roncaglione, William Morgan, Marshall Carper, William Lawton, and Walton Shepherd of the Medical Committee.

All of the case histories retold in this book are about real people in Charleston who have benefited from Preventive Care. Their names and vital information about their backgrounds have been dramatized so that no one story is about just one person, but rather each is a combination of facts about a lot of people who all reached the same conclusion—Preventive Care lifted their spirits and moved their bodies into a useful old age.

Medical data to prove the worth of low-mobility exercises will come later. Meanwhile, the Preventive Care program is here *now* to touch the lives of millions of older people and penetrate our society's "conspiracy of silence" that has surrounded them up to now.

Alice Hornbaker

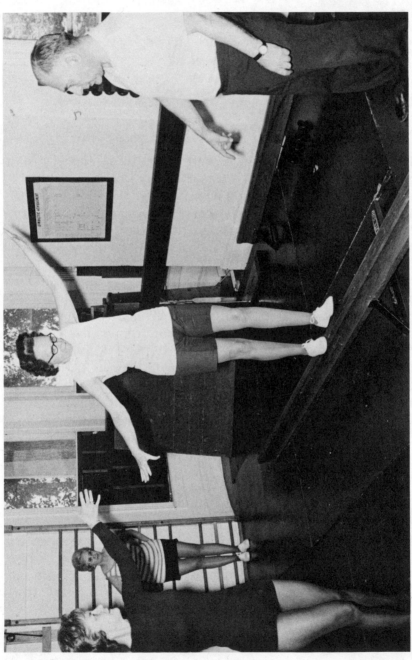

One of the early signs of aging is the shuffling, hesitant gait of older Americans. To reverse this, Lawrence Frankel recommends learning to walk a two-inch balance beam, demonstrated here. Betty Richard, left, and Frankel, right, assist woman in Preventive Care exercise class at Charleston, West Virginia, with her "solo."

Chapter 1

What Is Preventive Care?

TWO ELDERLY MEN, Sam and Harry, sat talking in the lobby of their apartment building. They had both just witnessed a demonstration of the Preventive Care exercise program staged by their peers. No one in it was under sixty-five.

Sam, nearing seventy, was against its concept. "I never exercised much in my whole life and nobody is going to make me do it now. No sir." As he spoke to his friend, his voice grew louder.

Harry, already eighty, was patient. He knew Sam was about to explode. He just waited for an opening to present his case—why he felt Lawrence Frankel had a good thing going for the elderly. He also had friends in that demonstration group. And they'd convinced him.

Sam raced on. His voice grew louder. "Why do you think so many people around here in this retirement housing development *are* still alive, Harry? Because they weren't damn fools, that's why. Exercise. Nuts."

"But Sam . . . ."

"That's it. That's all I got to say."

With that he raised his arm to signal he'd cut off his hearing aid, stood up, and marched off.

He never heard Harry's side of the argument. Too bad. It was Sam's loss. Harry later joined a Preventive Care class and is now considering enrolling in some college classes to learn a "second career." He's been seen lately, too, in the company of Eloise

19

Tyson, seventy, Apartment 101, one of his friends who had staged the demonstration for his fellow residents.

Sam had not only turned off his hearing aid when he didn't want his argument debated, but he had turned off his chance to live out the balance of his life with vitality and new meaning.

Lots of people over sixty-five, when first introduced to the new life-style, Preventive Care, balk.

One day, at a nursing home where Frankel and his "team," Mrs. Betty Byrd Richard, exercise instructor, and Mrs. Beulah Phillips, R.N., were going through their routine, Frankel noticed a new resident, a woman, watching intently.

Frankel went over to her. "Won't you join the circle and dance with us through these exercises?" he asked her.

"Nope."

"Why not? You walked in here, didn't you? I saw you keeping time to our music with your foot. You have rhythm."

"I never exercised much before. Mostly been a housewife, don't you know? I can't do those—those things the rest are doing."

"Certainly you can. If you want to. We'll help you. All of us want you to join the fun."

With that he took the lady's wrinkled hand, and like a gallant knight, led her into the circle for the dance-exercise routines.

After it was finished, Frankel escorted her back to her chair.

"See, that wasn't hard, was it?"

She giggled like a young girl. "Not bad at all. But maybe I'm just too old for all this, this activity."

"Wrong. Remember Sarah in the Bible?" Frankel had seen the woman carefully put her Bible down next to her when she got up to dance.

"Sarah, you know, was near ninety when she gave birth to a child."

He had hit a nerve. Her eyes twinkled. "That's right. Now, if more of these exercises make me feel this good, you can just find me a man and I'll see what I can do."

Frankel had won her over to Preventive Care.

I've talked to hundreds of others enrolled in Preventive Care exercise programs in Charleston. None of them were left untouched by its impact. Instead of talking about their arthritic hands or aching bones they were making plans to lunch together downtown, go to a concert or movie, listen to a lecture at the university. They were alive after sixty-five.

You can bring Preventive Care into your own life by learning at home the exercises shown and discussed in this book. Then, after you have achieved new mobility and endurance, you can be instrumental in forming a group Preventive Care class, expand your physical-fitness program, and start "living it up." You can break the stereotype mold, senior citizen, that society has cast you in. You can become a full first-class citizen who has something to contribute to society, retired or not.

Let's go, for a minute, to Charleston, the Shangri-la of physical fitness for the elderly. Let's see what happened there that's excited the whole nation into demanding similar programs in their home-towns.

Charleston, capital of West Virginia, is located in Kanawha Valley, an industrial complex of chemical-, glass-, and coal-oriented companies. It is largely white Anglo-Saxon with very few foreign ethnic groups and a small percentage of blacks. Approximately twenty thousand of Kanawha County's 250,000-plus population are over sixty-five.

Before the Lawrence Frankel Institute was founded in 1959, there were no recreational groups or clubs devoted to overt programs of preventive maintenance through guided exercise.

The Frankel Institute, which changed all of this, began as a private gym financed by professional, industrial, and business leaders who wanted directed physical exercise supervised by an expert—Lawrence Frankel. The same group wanted fitness and gymnastic classes for their children.

In 1960, because of a growing demand for additional programs for blind children, asthmatics, referred problems from local physicians, and a desire to enter into some research areas, the Lawrence Frankel Foundation, a nonprofit organization, was formed. It was incorporated in 1963. Offers of help poured in from local groups and individuals. The foundation's exercise programs for blind and asthmatic children were nationally reported. In 1963 the United States Public Health Service funded the foundation to study and report "Effects of Graded Exercise on Patients With Coronary Heart Disease."

The foundation also published several medical papers nationally on: (1) physical conditioning for asthmatic children; (2) ergometric evaluation of eighty-six physicians; (3) exercise and hypertension.

The private Frankel Institute and the public Frankel Foundation room together in an ancient building on the perimeter of downtown Charleston in a declining neighborhood. Situated at the corner of Virginia and Brooks Streets, the converted residence now houses a complete gymnasium and sauna, and has become the mecca for those who want to stay physically fit.

As Lawrence Frankel's reputation grew as an expert on physical fitness, his board of directors and the medical committee decided to expand their facilities to offer a program for the elderly, a heretofore ignored segment of the population when it came to physical-fitness regimens.

June 1, 1970, was the first day of the revolution. West Virginia's State Commission on Aging, excited about the foundation's proposal for exercise for the elderly, contracted with it to fund a pilot project for a year to study whether exercise decelerated aging.

With fifteen participants, ages sixty-five to ninety-three, divided between Lee Terrace Senior Citizen Resident Center (a high-rise apartment building) and Brooks Manor, a resident home for the elderly, Frankel's Preventive Care program began.

All participants had to have their doctor's approval in writing on file at foundation headquarters. This is the most important prerequisite of the Preventive Care program—permission of your doctor to do exercises, along with information about any cautions he feels you must observe. No one got into the classes without their doctor's okay—and blessing.

Obtaining the doctor's consent cast off a wonderful "by-product," for area physicians later admitted it alerted them for the first time to the physical-fitness needs of their elderly patients, something they hadn't given much thought to before. And it made them review their own needs. Many of these doctors became Preventive Care devotees themselves.

Before the classes actually began in the pilot project, an outline of the exercise regimens was presented for approval to the foundation's own medical-advisory committee. Unanimously they endorsed Frankel's plan.

What the pioneer fifteen participants did was to start with exercises of low-level, moderate intensity, designed to strengthen and tone their skeletal frame, jazz up their poor body mechanics and lack of flexibility, and lubricate the circulation of both the upper and lower limbs.

All participants had their heart rate and blood pressure measured both before the classes began and every two weeks thereafter.

Why?

Frankel wanted to have on record any improvements they showed in both heart function and breathing.

At the time the Frankel pilot project began, there were many other studies on physical activity and aging going on across the nation, including the program conducted at the famous Ethel Percy Andrus Gerontology Center located on the campus of the University of Southern California. This study was done by Dr. Herbert A. deVries. His pilot group, however, involved affluent men volunteers, in relatively good health and more oriented to physical activity than others in their peer groups.

The Preventive Care pioneers were both men *and* women, selected largely from *low*-income groups who admitted, "I never did any kind of sports before." Some even had medical problems such as heart disease or emphysema.

The school bell for exercise classes rang for the Preventive Care group each Monday, Wednesday, and Friday in two afternoon sessions. All were closly supervised and offered individual attention. Each group came to the foundation headquarters for an hour's workout. On Tuesdays and Thursdays the Frankel team, including Frankel, Betty Richard, and their nurse, Beulah Phillips, visited the elderly who were either not ambulatory or unable to come to the center.

After ten weeks in the program the pioneers were asked to take a second ergometer test. They were sent upstairs to Frankel's office where the ergometer bicycle stood. This demanding piece of equipment, a half-bike that's stationary, and the tests for it, are the brainchild of Dr. Olaf Astrand of Gymnastiska Centralinstitutet, Stockholm, Sweden. The bike and tests assess the physical fitness of a person by measuring graded work loads and giving an evaluation of the performance capacity possible of an individual. In other words, you ride the bike under a stress load to see what happens to your heart rate.

The Preventive Care pioneers originally did the ergometer bike test at the start of the pilot program. Frankel and his team used a metronome and two stopwatches, one to record work time, the other to measure heart rate. Changes of circulation and respiration were noted at rest, during, and after exercise.

They pedaled for six minutes, if they could. If their heart rate exceeded 120-125 beats per minute (Frankel took their pulse every minute for the six minutes they were on the bike) they had to stop.

The ten-weeks test proved what the foundation had hoped. All the pioneers improved both their strength and endurance for exercise.

"And besides," one lively woman of seventy-five reported, "it's fun. I haven't been on a bike since I was sixteen."

It took only a few months for the news to leak out that the Frankel Foundation program of Preventive Care was recycling old people into new. The word was, the pioneers could walk better, dance better, laugh more, cry less.

Preventive Care was working.

The initial program's funding ran out in 1971 and because it didn't have top priority in the state's budget, it was dropped. But the foundation's board of directors wanted it to go on. They knew they had a revolution on their hands. They sought public funds and got them. The program was expanded and today there are hundreds involved and more signing up each day.

In February, 1974, the Commission on Aging came back to Frankel with more state money to bring his program into the depressed neighborhoods ringing Charleston, where it is now being pursued. West Virginia wants Preventive Care for all of its citizens and then hopes to push the concept into national headlines.

And so the revolution grows. Like all radical ideas it had, at its beginning, only a small core of dedicated followers, and because of this no official government agency went overboard to endorse it. Many said the pilot group was too small. But the foundation was swamped with letters from all over the country wanting more information on how other cities and states could implement the program for their elderly.

You can help. Once you start your Preventive Care program in your own home, you'll be convinced of its worth. You'll probably want to join a group and expand the kinds of exercises you can do now. Then sit down and write your congressman. Seek Government money to fund Preventive Care programs in your community.

If Preventive Care in Charleston receives a national grant, it will enlarge its headquarters and begin to train "missionaries," men and women over fifty, to carry the program back to their areas (see Chapter 19).

But those who want to train as physical-education instructors must have rapport with the elderly, understand their fears as well as their joys, and relate to their needs. They will have to be able to reassure those they teach that exercise will enhance their lives, change their life-style, and make them want to go on living.

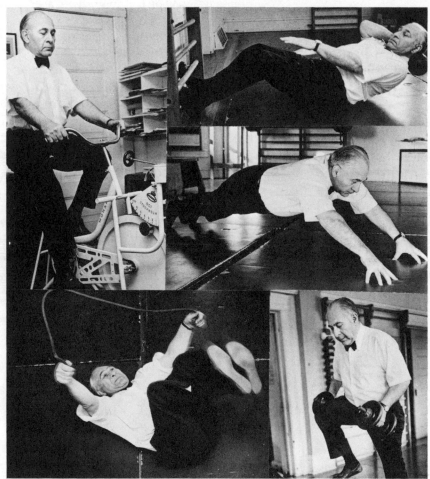

Going into his 70th year doesn't stop Lawrence Frankel from exercising. In the top left photo he tests himself on the bicycle ergometer, at high resistance, for several short intervals. In the top right photo the sit-up exercise is performed with a 60-pound dumbbell behind his neck. He does 8-10 repetitions to obtain the optimum abdominal muscle tone. In the top center photo Frankel shows how to do an arm push-up with arms fully extended, entire body supported between fingertips and toes. According to doctors, this exercise involves so many muscles and such vigorous effort it has been called "the test of a man." He does 15-20 repetitions two times weekly. At the lower left Frankel jumps rope while lying down on his back, a unique exercise for testing coordination. In the lower right photo Preventive Care's founder performs the step test on a 20-inch bench with a 25-pound dumbbell in each hand. This exercise is performed on an interval basis for two or three minutes, and following a rest it is repeated several times. The bicycle ergometer and the step tests are both cardio-respiratory exercises.

Chapter 2

Lawrence Frankel—He Cares

IN 1910 LITTLE BOYS in New York City dressed in romper suits. At least they did if they had a mother like Mama Frankel. She was born in Lithuania, immigrated to the United States, married, and had five children. She was devoted to her family, her kin, her neighbors. But her word was law.

Lawrence, a middle child, was designated by Mama that cold November morning to accompany her on a "special" trip. The six-year-old wore the hated "dress-up" suit. His hair was in the fashion for the times, a straight bob worn over the ears, with bangs. Big for his age, Lawrence was embarrassed by his outfit and didn't want to go.

"Get your coat," Mama said, "we go."

Their destination, which Frankel didn't know until they got there, was a home for the aged in lower Manhattan. All Mama had said was that they were going to visit a neighbor who'd come from Mama's village in the old country many years ago.

Mama and Lawrence entered the gloomy residence hall, quickly found the dormitory room where the Frankel's ex-neighbor was assigned, and hurried to her. Mama and the old lady fell into each other's arms, and amid the animated conversation, Lawrence was forgotten.

He didn't care. He had more than his share of curiosity for a six-year-old. The place was scary, quiet. His eyes went from one side of the huge room to the other as he tried to count the beds. In each of them was a time-spent old lady. Most of them were either lying down or sitting up along the side, staring. There was no conversation between them.

Lawrence tried not to stare, a habit his mother warned him about. But he couldn't help it. The place seemed so unreal. There was nothing to distinguish that living people stayed there. No personal effects, no flowers, no joy.

But one bit of action did fascinate Lawrence. He noticed each occupant performed a little ritual every now and then. From a brown paper bag the old ladies would withdraw scraps of bread, push the food quickly into their toothless mouths. They seemed very hungry.

Lawrence waited until he and Mama were safely outside of the gloomy home before he asked, "Mama, what are all of those old ladies doing in that great big room?"

Mama was silent. She grabbed Lawrence's hand, lost in thought. Together they pushed against the strong winter wind and walked rapidly toward home. Mama's grip on Lawrence made him wince.

Since she didn't respond to the question, the six-year-old pursued. "Mama, didn't you hear? What were those old ladies *doing* there?"

Mama Frankel stopped, looked down at her son, and said, "They are there because they're old. Their children don't want them any more. They have been deserted in their old age."

They started walking again. Lawrence tugged at his mother's coat, made her stop, and looking up into her eyes, cried, "Mama, I won't ever, ever let anything like that happen to you."

And he didn't. All through his life, and until his mother died in her eighties, Frankel was her devoted son. Not because he had to be, or should be, but because he wanted to be.

However, the specter of that little scene in that dungeonlike home for the aged haunted him for years. He feared not for his own parents, who were loved and revered until their deaths, but for all the others who were scrapped and left to die.

Now Lawrence, at sixty-nine, has dedicated the remainder of his life to eradicating his private ghost and break the "conspiracy of silence" toward the largest growing minority in the world—those over sixty-five.

Today there are more than 20 million Americans over sixty-five and the number is growing. Since Americans are having less children, the age of the average citizen is rising. Predictions are by the year 2000 more than half the population will be over fifty and one-third of it will be over sixty-five.

Everyone—you in your twenties, you at forty, and you at fifty-five—must join this "minority" someday. That's where the real generation gap is. The young don't relate to the old *as a group they'll be joining.* If and when they do relate, then all citizens, young and old alike, will share in the activity of mainstream living.

Lawrence Frankel wants to act as the catalyst to help every American now not physically fit and over sixty-five to "recycle."

"I didn't plan on making physical fitness my profession," Frankel told me. "In 1930 after attending both Columbia and New York Universities, where I studied business, I came to Charleston to manage a group of department stores for my older brother.

"Having always been active in school sports, especially gymnastics, I soon visited the Charleston YMCA to see if I could use their gymnastic equipment to stay in shape. To my surprise I found that the city YMCA offered only swimming and basketball. The gymnastic equipment had long since rusted away, unused."

That situation was easily overcome by the man now known in Charleston as the high priest of exercise. He personally raised money to buy new gym equipment and became the Y's volunteer instructor in small, informal classes in gymnastics.

For twenty years Lawrence served as the Y's physical-fitness director. He had to act out the role of successful businessman during his daytime hours. But when his store closed Lawrence almost ran to his beloved gym. Like the Clark Kent of his day who became Superman with a change of clothes, Lawrence went from conservative business suit to his most comfortable attire, gym clothes. In his prime Lawrence weighed two-hundred pounds, distributed over a musclar five foot, ten inch frame. Today he's even five pounds lighter than in his youth.

Amazing feats of strength often were performed by Frankel in the gym, not to extol his own strength, but to encourage more and more Charleston men and boys to try physical fitness as a way of life. On his fortieth brithday, in 1945, Lawrence celebrated the occasion by proving to his young charges that he was indeed "not over the hill," as a few had suggested. While his class watched, Lawrence grabbed the stall bars and slowly raised himself out until he was parallel to the floor. He held this position for four seconds—with a 110-pound weight strapped to his waist.

"Wow," whistled one of the youngsters. He went home and told his dad. The word got round and someone wrote up the incident and sent it to famous columnist Ripley, who had a sketch drawn of Lawrence. It ran in the February, 1946 edition in his syndicated "Believe It or Not" newspaper featurette, circulated around the world. Three years earlier Lawrence had performed a similar feat wearing a fifty-pound barbell strapped to his waist. That had been reported in John Hix's nationwide column "Strange As It Seems."

So to his boys at the gym Lawrence proved you don't get older, you get better.

"Muscles in themselves don't mean anything," Frankel would tell his awe-struck audience of junior boys, who nicknamed him Superman. "I don't recommend muscular training merely to develop big muscles. I believe in mentality over muscles. There is no need for brawn without brainpower. Brute strength is nothing."

As Lawrence's interest in physical fitness grew, so did his reputation for teaching others. He read books on anatomy, kinesiology, and exercise physiology. His brother, Dr. Charles Frankel, associate professor of orthopedics at the University of Virginia, helped him in his thirst for knowledge of the human body.

Frankel started what became an international correspondence with doctors who specialized in physical fitness. Authorities such as the late Dr. Paul Dudley White, Dr. Hans Kraus, Dr. Olaf Astrand of Sweden, Dr. David Brunner of Israel, Dr. Ernest Jokl, Dr. Herbert deVries, and others influenced his thinking.

"I started designing exercise programs while teaching at the Y. Somebody with a problem such as bad posture would approach me and ask for my help.

"With his doctor's approval I would plan a series of therapeutic exercises. Soon I gained a reputation for helping people through these programs and many requests came for help. Mildly handicapped individuals were referred to me by doctors. I worked with people recuperating from surgery and others just wishing to learn skills such as judo and boxing. [Frankel taught both to Charleston's police force.] I continued communicating by letter with specialists, relating my experiences and asking them questions when problems arose."

Then a funny thing started happening around Charleston. After World War II large numbers of people of all ages flocked to Frankel's Y classes to learn how to change their way of life to his.

One of the stories Charlie Connor, managing editor of Charleston's *Daily Mail* newspaper, told all over town in 1954 concerned Lawrence. In the column he then wrote, "Roving the Valley;" Charlie reported that there was a standing offer to buy a new suit of clothes for any officer on the state police force or in the sheriff's office who could lift the special hand-grip apparatus in Lawrence Frankel's back office. The catch was, it weighed 650 pounds.

Four hands against Lawrence's two weren't uncommon in Charleston as muscle men, including professional football players and wrestlers, came in to try to lift the weight. No one did. Except Frankel. And he did it on command.

Lawrence built the device not to win bets or build muscles (with a forty-seven-inch chest, who needed it?) but as his personal safety factor—to keep from breaking his neck. He needed grip power.

"While I was a kid I did a 'giant swing' on a horizontal bar, lost my grip, and fell twenty-five feet to the floor. Others in the gym advised me not to attempt gymnastics. 'They're for slender fellows, not brawny guys like you.'

"It was good advice," he recalled, "but I loved working out on apparatus so much I knew I couldn't give it up. So I sent away for this hand-gripping machine. I started out to build up my grip so I could continue gymnastic work. I began at two-hundred pounds and gradually built up to the 630 pounds now holding the bars apart."

The apparatus was set up in the back room in Lawrence's department store and became an instrument of frustration for all of Charleston's strongest men.

No one ever won that free suit of clothes.

It did reinforce Lawrence's contention that a strong grip could save a man's life. "That was proven at Pearl Harbor when a lot of men lost their lives because they didn't have enough strength in their hands to climb up ropes thrown to them after their ships sank. After that every high-school and college-gym class in America was given instructions to teach rope climbing."

Lawrence continued selling apparel in his department store by day and teaching physical fitness at night. Then, in 1932 he met a woman named Dorothy, a pretty blonde who became the first person in his adult life to "throw" him. They were married in 1939.

Dorothy was the first to see that Lawrence's "double" professions, selling by day and teaching physical education classes by night, were taxing even his super strength. But she knew how much he loved his Y classes so she kept silent.

Frankel enlarged his scope of knowledge, now branching into programs for the handicapped. During the 1950's a Charleston allergist came to Lawrence with a special request.

"Lawrence, asthmatic kids need exercise, too. Can you fit a program to their needs?"

He said yes.

"We wanted the children in our asthmatic exercise program to be as active as possible, so we placed equal emphasis on the physical and breathing exercises. I designed a group of exercises that included workouts with Roman Rings, horizontal bars, medicine ball, rope climbing, swimming, tumbling, and other gymnastics. We also taught children basic skills of boxing and judo."

The class, later named by the children themselves as "Bucking Broncos" (children bucking bronchial asthma), became famous. A story about them appeared in the December 13, 1958 issue of the *Journal of the American Medical Association,* and nationwide newspaper features. Later a pharmaceutical company made a documentary of the project and distributed it internationally. Before long, other programs like the Bucking Broncos sprang up in cities across the nation.

Lawrence's two lives had their moment of truth in the late 1950's when he met Dr. Ernest Jokl, professor of Physiology at University of Kentucky and president of UNESCO's Council of Physical Education and Sport. They became instant friends.

One day, after a particularly enlightening exchange of knowledge, Jokl asked Frankel, "What are you doing in the world of business?"

He couldn't answer. But the question served as the alchemist that solved his conflict of interests between business and physical fitness as professions. He told his wife how much he wanted to organize health-oriented and cardio-protective programs, and to make them available not just to the young, but to people of all ages in his communtiy.

Instead of fighting him, Dorothy asked, "What took you so long?"

In 1959 Lawrence liquidated his businesses and together with a group of interested men started the Foundation and Fitness Center at Virginia and Brooks Streets. He was its director and the stockholders were the board of directors. They outfitted the center with three gyms, the latest in equipment, and a sauna bath.

Before anyone could participate in the gym programs, he had to bring to the center the written consent of his doctor. Since doctors were on the board, a separate medical committee was formed to advise Frankel and help him with individualized programs for members.

Many projects followed. In 1960 the center received nationwide attention when it initiated a gymnastic program for blind children. It was among the first in the country, and medical journals and newspapers across the land wrote about it. For the first time these children lost their fear of exercising.

When Lawrence and his board got the grant from the Government to study the effects of exercise on men who had suffered heart attacks, specialists poured into Charleston to participate in symposiums on physical fitness. The reputation of Lawrence Frankel grew.

In 1970 he had his chance to implement his lifelong dream of helping the elderly live better lives. He found himself thinking more and more of that day, long ago in 1910, when he had seen what effects inactivity and lack of human care and concern had on old people. He could hear himself saying, to his mother, "Not you, Mama, not ever. I'll never let it happen to you."

But all around Lawrence in Charleston there was evidence that a lot of sons and daughters had let their parents down. He saw too many of them doomed to finish their lives shut up in those warehouses for the dying—nursing homes. No zest for life. No dignity. Nothing.

"Yet, the Government was subsidizing thousands of nursing homes at a profit to their owners. They didn't care about the people living in them. Only the profit was important. I knew then I had to do something to reverse that trend."

His plan was to use his thirty years experience in physical fitness to design supervised and individualized exercise to slow down the aging process and to prove it works, for when people feel good again, they become mentally alert, too. There would be greatly diminished need for nursing homes, and the Government money could go instead into preventive medicine and care. Thus Preventive Care was born.

In the programs that followed, and even today, Lawrence Frankel goes to the people who can't come to him. He, and his team, help those in all stages of physical mobility. If they are in wheelchairs, he gives them special exercises they can do sitting down. If they are arthritic, he gives them muscle builders. They can do their exercises at the foundation headquarters, or in classes where they live, and yes, even in nursing homes. But, for these people, Frankel's help comes at the eleventh hour.

"We are there earlier than we could have been, but later than we should have been," Lawrence said.

The exercises in Preventive Care programs are all done to music. Lawrence maintains it enhances both mood and tolerance.

"Any music with a decided beat can be used while you do your daily routines," Frankel said. "We like soothing music, beautiful music, but with enough bounce so you can spring into your exercises with enthusiasm."

Not a militant man ordinarily, Lawrence becomes almost so when he thinks about all the money the Government is putting into Medicare programs, including tons of literature nobody reads. He maintains that if only a trickle of that money went to rehabilitating old people and those in pre-retirement years, it could save the Government millions of tax dollars. The government then would be practicing Preventive Care—not Medicare.

"My ambition is to involve as many of our older citizens as possible in active, viable programs, already proven to decelerate the aging process. I want to demonstrate on a mass scale, now, that there is no age at which exercise will not be of benefit."

Grace is important in any stage of life, but in Preventive Care classes it is stressed. Participants are encouraged to work out dance routines to music, to pep up circulation and have fun doing it.

Chapter 3

Black is Beautiful—Hattie Clay

AT FIFTY-TWO HATTIE MAE CLAY thought she had it made. And, if she did, it was mostly because she willed it so.

Born into a black ghetto neighborhood in Charleston, Hattie had had her share of troubles in her younger days, just staying alive. But she raised a fine son, "Got him grown and out of this here town and 'down' neighborhood—into another state," and life seemed good.

Most of her neighbors knew Hattie as the best beautician around. Not only did she own her own shop, she had two others working for her. They had more business than they could handle. So in 1950, working six days a week, combining a widow's pension with her shop profits, there didn't seem to be a cloud in Hattie Mae's sky.

That Saturday in 1950 things in the shop were moving. Hattie's deft fingers combed out one hair style after another. But by 3 P.M. she became a clock watcher. She felt tired. Really tired. But, like always, she sang, made jokes, and kidded with her customers.

"Lord, Hattie Mae, what makes you so cheerful on such a rotten day?" one customer asked.

"Got nothing to be 'down' about, Maybelle. I learned long ago only to look 'up.' Now you take my Henry, God rest his soul, he was nothin' but a 'down' person. He never saw no good in nothin'—not me, not Jimmy, our boy, nothin.' But you gotta listen to the Lord, Maybelle. He'll make you want to sing all the time."

"Hey, Hattie, save the preaching for down the street, will ya? I got a big night tonight. So let's get me outta here."

37

Hattie wasn't squelched. She'd taken a lot of ribbing about her faith. "Never liked gossipin' crowds none. Stayed away from all that cardplaying and smoking bunch, too." Hattie's neighbors claimed they could set their clocks on Sunday by watching her race past them on the way to church. She walked like she was always five minutes late.

"Yes, yes," she singsonged to herself now. "This life has been good enough to me."

That was the last thing Hattie remembered saying that day.

The next thing she recalled was the moment she opened her eyes and found herself flat on her back, mute, in a hospital ward full of noisy people. Hovering over her were two doctors and a nurse. They kept calling her name. Didn't they know she *wanted* to answer? Her eyes pleaded for help. But not a sound would come out.

"Hattie, can you hear me? Hattie, you've had a stroke."

Hattie stared at the voice. She tried to lift her left arm but nothing moved. Not the arm, not the fingers. And the left leg was dead, too.

"I remember crying silently to myself, Oh Lord, why have you done this to me? I'm on your side, Lord. Why me? Why now?"

Hattie thought she was going to die but the doctors reassured her—or tried to. They kept saying she'd get better.

But she didn't. Not for a long time. She stayed on in that hospital ward for months to receive only token care. No one ordered physical therapy nor were there any attempts to help her up and walk.

"But I wasn't bitter. Not then, not now. I've been doing for myself all of my life and I wasn't going to quit. I decided one day I'd just have to help myself if I wanted to get well. My speech returned soon after the stroke so at least I could tell my friends who visited me what I wanted them to do.

"I had them tie strips of old cloth to the headboard of my bed, long enough for me to grip with my good arm. Then I'd practice trying to pull myself up. I'd wrap the cloth around my left arm and try to use it, too. Lord, it hurt. But I knew I had to keep moving—or die."

Walking was another major goal. Hattie waited for help. None came. One day she rolled off her bed onto the floor. By now her weight had increased thirty pounds from inactivity, so she took a jolt when she landed. Then she'd try to sit up. She got bawled out by the floor nurse for leaving her bed.

"Didn't matter none. The next day they'd find me right back on the floor, exercising, trying to sit up, to move my legs together. Pretty soon I did. Then I asked for a walker. With it, I took my first steps, alone."

When Hattie was discharged from the hospital she *walked* out. Her left leg dragged, she leaned heavily on a cane, but she went out, on her own. Her left arm functioned at half-efficiency, and her fingers not at all.

"I went back to my little home which, thank the Lord, I owned outright. I started doing for myself. My boy, Jimmy, he wanted to come home, live with me, take care of me. 'No sir,' I told him, 'you've got a good life right where you are. Stay put. I'm not the first mother to have a stroke. Won't be the last. I can't set hair no more but I'll manage.' "

Hattie did keep the shop for a few more years, letting the operators do the work while she managed the business. But it was hard—eventually she had to sell out. Then urban renewal came to her neighborhood, forced Hattie to sell her home, too. She went to live in a Government apartment building designed for the ghetto's refugees over sixty-five.

"The apartment was no different from my own home. It needed me and I needed it. So long as I kept moving, nothing hurt too much. You just gotta make yourself do things when you get old.

"I'd pretend when I got bored that I had an appointment to go somewhere. I'd get dressed by 10 A.M. and drag these old bones down to a city bus. Then I'd ride crosstown and back. Sometimes I'd get off and walk around to see new things, new faces.

"Weren't never a day I couldn't find something to do, something to smile over. I told my child that same thing. Be an 'up' person and you can always manage. But my leg still wasn't much good to me."

Where Hattie lives, there are many retired people rocking out the balance of their years in limbo.

"They don't move, they don't walk, and most of the time they don't even talk," Hattie said. "They just sit and rot. That's not for me.

"You know, God told us to take care of ourselves. You do that and

He'll watch over you. Every time Jesus healed the lame and made them well or cured the blind and made them see, He then told them to pick up their beds and walk. He didn't tell them to go sit down. Don't you take that as a message that everyone is supposed to move around?"

When a Preventive Care group in Hattie's age bracket came to her apartment building in 1972 to demonstrate exercises of low mobility for the aged, Hattie was ready for them. She was, at seventy-four, the first to say 'yes' because she already knew the value of exercise. And maybe, just maybe, down at Preventive Care they'd find a way to help her loosen up her bad leg.

Hattie approached Frankel and told him she'd like to come.

"I had this here stroke twenty-two years ago, you know?" she told him. "Left me with this bad leg and arm. Even my face never came untwisted. But I can do for myself just fine."

"Come," Frankel told her.

And Hattie did. The very next class that met, Hattie was there. She had to take a city bus and walk the rest of the way, but she showed up, and on time. After six months of group exercise Hattie, for the first time since her stroke, gave up her cane. She now walks without it.

"Look here," she pointed to her left hand. "Even it works much better now since Mr. Frankel prescribed some finger and hand exercises. There's life in this old gal yet. And she likes to ex-er-cise."

What did Hattie's doctor say about her, at seventy-four returning to an exercise class?

"He signed the consent slip right off," Hattie said. "He told me if it got me out of the house, and back in with lots of people who liked to do more things than listen to their arteries harden, then I should do it."

"I like being here in this here class. I do what I can with all the exercises but I like best to talk to all these people. We don't cry here about our aches and pains. No—Mr. Frankel wouldn't allow that. We talk about 'up' things."

Hattie, more than ever, equates life in terms of "up" and "down" people. Her late husband was "down," but the Preventive Care people are "up," like her son.

"My faith has kept me going this long," Hattie said. "I believe

He wants us all to exercise and stay strong. And if He had to put stumbling blocks in our path, then it was to make us stronger."

When Hattie sits on her exercise mat, doing stretches and bends, you know it's got to hurt. But she does them. And when they do a routine she just can't push her overweight frame into, she sits up, watches the others, and calls out, over the music that always plays for the routines, "Keep at it. That's right. Love your heart."

Everyone in the class loves Hattie. For them she exemplifies black is beautiful.

Bend down, if you want to get thin. Classes in *Preventive Care* instruct older Americans in a wide variety of exercises, including the old-fashioned bend-down-and-touch-your-toes.

Chapter 4

"The Blind Shall Lead Them"

LUCY PACED UP and down in front of her modest Charleston home, tapping out a sort of cadence with her white cane. It was her day to attend exercise class with the Preventive Care group at Carroll Terrace. Usually she waited for her taxicab to drive up to the curb before she came down off the graceful front veranda. It was just a short ride to the apartment building where the classes were held twice a week but without "sighted" help, she couldn't get there.

Today it was unseasonably beautiful. Midwinter and warm. She couldn't suppress the urge to get out into the springlike day and feel the warmth from the sun.

The cab was late so Lucy just paced back and forth, counting the steps so she wouldn't stray too far from her front yard and maybe miss the cab.

Suddenly she felt a strong bump. An angry voice, young and gruff, apologized; someone picked up Lucy's cane and handed it back to her.

"It's all right," Lucy said.

Instead of being contrite, the woman hurried away, calling back, "Why don't you blind people look where you're going?"

"I laughed so. I couldn't wait to tell somebody else about it."

When the taxi did come and the driver heard Lucy's story, he swore.

"Don't take it so seriously," she said to him. "I personally think it's pretty funny."

The driver eased into the curb in front of a modern, glass exterior high-rise apartment building. Its façade was bright, new, young-looking. No one would guess that inside there were more than 215 old people, most of whom were, by inactivity, tethered into an isolation of their own making.

"Here, wait a minute," the driver said, racing to the back door, "let me help you out."

"That's real nice of you, young man. But all the drivers know that once I'm here I can handle myself real well. But thank you for your concern."

Lucy apologized to her class for being so late. The others, who ranged in age from sixty-seven to eighty-four, were already limbering up.

Lucy found a chair, took off her coat, laid down her cane, and strode confidently to the front of the class to call out the exercises, replacing Preventive Care instructor, Betty Richard.

The first time Lucy came to this class she was not this confident.

"I always had a pretty good sense of rhythm," Lucy recalled, "but I was afraid I couldn't follow the intricate patterns they might use.

"I had first heard about the foundation's program while attending a club meeting for a blind association in Charleston. An announcement was read there. Some of our members were already retired, and getting pretty fat. I thought it sounded good, too, but I didn't do anything about it then.

"Later, after I had to retire from my job as a vendor saleswoman because of poor health, I finally found the courage to call Mr. Frankel.

"I'm blind," I told him. "But I do want to tone up with exercises. I have no self-discipline to do anything here at home. But I think I might in a class situation. Besides, I need a reason to get out of doors."

"Can you get transportation to class?"

"Yes, a taxi will bring me to the door. It's such a short way, it wouldn't cost much."

"Then we'll expect you."

"It was just as simple as that," Lucy remembered. "I discussed it with my husband again and he was still all for it.

"But then he always is. He's handicapped, too, you see. Harry was born with cerebral palsy but it never stopped him from doing what he wanted to do. He really understands people, even without you talking. He's the wonder of my life."

The exercise class is one of the few places Lucy goes without her husband at her side. Both of them regularly attend church, professional meetings, outings of all kinds—always together.

"He's my eyes."

"When others say, 'How can you two manage so well?' we kind of draw back because we aren't trying to do anything special. Just get along. If it inspires others, fine. But that's not why we do it. We both had major adjustments to make with life. We've learned to cope. So when we do something it's always just because we want to."

And Lucy wanted to exercise. Although she is tall—five feet, eight inches—she now has a real weight problem. When she worked full time she was more active and watched her diet. But sitting at home alone during the day made her prone to snacking. Since she began the class exercises, though, she's trimmed off twenty pounds. "I feel like I can move around again, want to do more things like before."

The first time Lucy appeared in the Preventive Care class everyone predicted disaster. When Betty called out a new exercise, those on either side of Lucy expected a swat in the mouth. Lucy's arms windmilled.

Betty saw her dilemma.

As the music accelerated the pace, Betty left the front of the room and walked behind Lucy. She whispered into Lucy's ear, "Just listen to the music as I talk the exercises to you. I'll put my arms over yours and you can feel the patterns."

Lucy felt them, learned them, and went on to lead them for others, all sighted.

Actually, Lucy was always an extrovert. Her blindness wasn't congenital and it wasn't until she was eight years old that her parents realized she was losing her sight. Despite medical help, it grew worse in her adolescence.

"I sure had some bad years in-between the growing panic of darkness and the day it finally arrived and I was totally blind. And after that, for almost five years, I just didn't want to live."

Lucy's family threw a protective shield around her for a decade.

But they saw that this was destroying Lucy's initiative to do anything for herself. They feared for the day when they'd be gone and she had no one to care for her. So when they heard about a new program in Charleston, offered by a blind organization that was teaching blind people to be vendor salespeople, and then got them jobs, her parents insisted Lucy go to the city for the opportunity.

"The lady who trained me as a vendor to work in stands in the federal buildings was as new at her job as I was at being alone. She cried. She said she was afraid of me. I told her I was just as afraid and we'd learn together. That's the secret of reaching people. She cared. I cared. Together we learned. I suddenly felt useful again. But I had to wait almost a year for a job opening up full time. Until then I substituted, got really sharp.

"Then I got a call. A permanent job in a Federal building. There's where I met Harry. His voice told me he was kind. His gait told me he was handicapped. But what wonderful eyes he had—he saw for the both of us. I knew I'd at last found a man I could love who loved me back. We were married three months later—on Christmas Eve.

"Now that I've had to retire, it's only Harry who works. I find I have to force myself to keep active. It's so easy to just let yourself go."

She smiled. "But I won't because my husband says he doesn't like fat women."

Lucy does all of her own housework and cooking, and has a woman come in only once a month to do heavy cleaning.

"I'm a good cook, too." Lucy said. "The only bad thing I ever did was once I used salt instead of sugar in a cake. My husband kidded me about that for years. Said I should send the recipe in to the Pillsbury contest. He's a tease."

While we talked, a classmate came up to Lucy and complimented her new curly hairdo.

Lucy replied, "You sound pretty today, too."

Lucy's like that. Cheerful. Involved. A joy to be around.

"I heard on a radio newscast the other night that by the year 2000 scientists predict aging will be conquered," she told me.

I told her, yes, they were working on a solution in the labs around the world.

"But don't they realize that we've *got* the answer right here? One we can do something about *now*? I won't be around in the year 2000. I only wish more of the elderly in this very building would come down here and grow younger with us."

Part of the fun of Preventive Care is bringing its regimens to others in demonstrations. Here Charleston's older citizens, ages sixty to ninety-two, show off their agility for the city's invited onlookers. Music always is played to enhance both mood and tolerance.

Chapter 5

Francie and Johnny Were Lovers

LIVING IN AN activity-void home for the elderly can be a drag—
especially if you're ninety-two, vigorous, and a former traveling
salesman with so many good stories to tell the tongue can hardly
keep up.

John Leigher was all of those things. When a new home for the
elderly was announced in the paper, complete with pictures, it
sounded good to him. John decided to move in. Up until then he
had, at ninety, maintained his own place. But, since the last of his
family was gone now, it got to be lonely. And John loved people.
So he thought the home would be good because someone else
would cook and serve his meals and do his housekeeping. He'd
meet new friends. It seemed like a solution to his problem of
isolation.

"At first it was boring. Most of the old men here did nothing but
complain about their illnesses, real or otherwise. But *I* felt good.
Since I loved to talk I wanted an exchange of ideas. No one else did.
It was discouraging, so I kind of started keeping to myself more
and more. I wasn't finding the companionship I'd hoped for.

"Then Francie came. Things picked up right away. That southern belle had more kind words and good fun in her than all the rest
of them in this place had, including the administration. We just
naturally gravitated toward one another."

Or so he thought. But long before Francie and Johnny were "an
item" at the home, Francie had picked John out as her man. Six
months before she had seen John's pictures in the daily news-

paper. He was shown demonstrating the Preventive Care exercises. It was at a luncheon of the local Kiwanis Club in Charleston.

"That man is for me," she told her daughter, who was visiting her that week.

Francie sold her home in Charleston and she, too, moved into this home for the elderly. But she wasn't after meals on time or clean rooms. She wanted John.

The day after she was settled, Francie went looking for him. His favorite "sitting place" was a plush green velvet loveseat, near the piano. He always sat near any kind of music. He loved it so. Sometimes someone in the home would play the piano. Other times he'd just listen to the radio. And the couch also was a vantage point to announce to the others in the home when the Frankel team was coming. That was the highlight of his week.

Sitting there, in his white suit, immaculately groomed, he looked like a dwarf-sized Colonel Sanders. His full head of hair, trim white mustache, and slight goatee, made him a natural for a TV commercial. All he needed was a mint julep in his hand.

Francie introduced herself to him with: "Folks around here say you're stuck up? Are you?"

John retorted, "Hell, no." They both laughed. The romance blossomed.

John explained: "I was never snobbish to anyone else here. It's just that we couldn't talk. I liked doing the exercises and then I felt so good I wanted to have some fun—talk, tell jokes, laugh. The rest of them didn't. At least not at first. Francie made some of them want to. She's the kindest woman here. Why she'll walk those 'confused ones' up and down the hall, sing to them, run errands. She brought us all joy."

And exercise. Francie personally went to each room to literally pull bodies from their rockers and beds and urge them into the lounge to try Preventive Care.

"Most of them didn't even want to try," Francie said. "At first we had just a few. But later on, the class grew. The problem here was many took lots of medicines, and it kind of dulled them. But after awhile a lot of them stopped that stuff. One old lady told me she hadn't taken a sleeping pill for six weeks since she started exercising with us."

"Francie's mainly responsible for that. She just won't take no for an answer unless she knows they are really ill."

"John, how you go on," Francie said, covering his hand with hers. But she was obviously pleased at his compliment. It made everyone feel good just watching them laugh and tease each other like teenagers one minute, then be quietly kind and loving the next.

We were talking while the Preventive Care class was in progress. John had to beg off because of a bout with the flu. But when the sounds of "Alley Cat" started up, he turned to Francie, pinched her, and said, "Get up there and show this lady how well you dance."

"Oh, John. Oh. All right. But you know *he's* the dancer. Really light on his feet. I guess he must have danced his way through every city in the Southeast at one time. Did you know he was still selling men's clothing when he was eighty-five?"

John pushed her to get up.

Francie joined the circle with her friends, but kept looking back over her shoulder at her man. He smiled each time.

John had time to talk some more about the dilemma facing those in a home like this who still enjoy good health and *can* exercise.

"Time is our biggest enemy here," he told me. "These exercise classes have been wonderful because they make you feel alive. But then there's nothing to do to channel that new energy into worthwhile activity. I miss that. I could still sell. Sometimes I have a mind to get out of here. But then I'd lose Francie. . . ."

When I suggested forming discussion groups, perhaps finding volunteer work they could do from inside the home for the community, his eyes sparkled.

"I'd like that. Nothing ages a person faster than a dull mind."

Panting, Francie came back to the couch to be with Johnny. She picked up on his theme.

"I play the piano for the residents here sometimes. And for John. Most of the people want to hear hymns. They're all right but not a challenge for an accomplished musician like me. I prefer the classics. So does John."

"But a swing tune never hurt the ears one bit either," John added.

"You're right. But we'd love to have concerts held up here.

Maybe groups of students from the university. And a chance to get out of here more often and do something worthwhile. I do need more to do."

"Easy, old lady. You'll have her convinced we're becoming dull."

Neither of them were that. Their mature love set them apart from the others.

Yes, Francie and Johnny were lovers. At the home they had found new hope in each other. Preventive Care had brought them together. Now both were leaders in the program to get others to perk up, be alert, and think about a new life of activity.

Chapter 6

My God! I'm Having a Heart Attack!

WHEN HANK AND Mary Goodall left the high-school basketball game Frank was exhilarated. His alma mater had won. Howie, his son, was high scorer with twenty-two points. The boy's name bounced off the walls of the gym throughout the evening.

"Wow, it's pouring," Hank said as he pushed open the exit door. He turned to his wife, Mary, and asked her to wait while he brought the car around. With giant strides he crossed the parking lot quickly. Then he squeezed into his son's compact car (Howie had traded cars with him because he had a big date after the game) and returned to pick up his wife.

"Great game, wasn't it Mary? Howie's a cinch for a full basketball scholarship now. He's good!"

Flushed with pride, Mary snuggled close to her husband, trying not to break her personal, warm spell of delight. "He looked like you out there, Hank. I almost cried remembering."

They weren't more than three blocks from the school when the pain hit.

Suddenly Hank found himself short of breath. It seemed as though his chest was in the grip of a huge hand, determined to close its fist and squeeze the life from him.

He tried to relax, breathe deeply. Another stabbing pain. Then it hit his left shoulder, ran down his arm. Hank turned to Mary, his voice alarmed.

"My God, Mary, I can hardly breathe. Something's wrong. There's pain. . . ."

53

You're never too old for Preventive Care exercises. Here a ninety-year-old man goes through his routine with a smile on his face.

Mary pushed away from him—startled by the sound of his voice. "What pain . . . What's the matter?"

But before she could ask another question, Hank jerked the car toward the curb, cut the ignition. He slumped toward Mary's shoulder.

"It's . . . I . . . think . . . I'm having a heart attack. Get around . . . come to my side. Drive. Get me to a hospital.

Mary sped across town to the hospital's emergency entrance, raced inside to summon help. Two attendants came back with her and carried Hank in a stretcher to the coronary unit. He was still conscious, almost afraid to breathe. The admitting doctor warned him not to move to avoid another seizure.

Mary paced the length of the waiting room, aware of all the sounds around her—the murmur of other people's troubles, the infusion of doctors' reassurances, the laughter of a young nurse. Finally it was her turn. Their family doctor came toward her, his face marked with anxiety.

He took her hand into his and said, "Yes, Mary, Hank was right. He had a severe heart attack. I have a specialist with him now. We can go in to him for a minute. He wants to see you. But, please, Mary, try not to show your fear. We can't upset him now."

Hank was still conscious. He looked at his wife, his doctor, and the stranger at his bedside. He knew. Tears collected in Mary's eyes, hit her cheek. She blinked hard to erase them, but it only pumped up the flow.

"Hank. Mary's here. And this is Dr. Kalan, a specialist. You're in good hands. We've got everything under control. We want you to sleep now. Mary will be nearby."

All Mary could do was nod her head, too afraid to speak. Hank closed his eyes.

During the next three weeks in the hospital, first in intensive care, and later in convalescence, Hank, in his mind's eye, played out his life in review. Over and over it ran. I'm fifty-five years old. Ex-athlete. Successful real-estate broker. Wife who cares. Three sons, the youngest headed for big college basketball. Financially sound. Candidate for a heart attack? No. Yes. Well, sure, maybe. Who isn't? But not as likely as some others. Yet, it's happened. Sure, the last ten years have been my busiest. Not much time for anything else. Weight's got away from me. I'm over 240 pounds. Drink lots more than I used to.

Around and around he played the kaleidoscope of his life. His head pounded out the same final question, "But what am I going to do—*now?*"

One Sunday Hank was especially restless. No visitors yet. Too early. The Sunday paper was scattered over his bed and tray as he tried to read, to concentrate. As he browsed the Sunday magazine supplement, a headline caught his eye. It read: "Make Your Heart Exercise."

It was the story of the Frankel Foundation's government-funded project to determine the amount and kind of exercise men could take who had recently undergone heart attacks.

"Why, they mean me." Reading the article thoroughly Hank knew he *had* to get into that exercise class.

Monday he called Lawrence Frankel, was assured that as soon as he had his doctor's permission after his release from the hospital, there would be a place for him in the exercise program.

Three weeks after he was out of the hospital, in May, 1964, Goodall started into the program. He's been exercising ever since, even now that he is retired and into the Preventive Care program.

"Exercise has become a way of life for me," Hank said. "I didn't want to be one of those heart patients who spent the balance of his life limiting his physical activity to a walk to the corner or an occasional round of golf."

Every week, except for vacations, Hank visits the gym three days a week. He is now sixty-five.

His routine at the Preventive Care center and gym includes work at the special exercise bench created by Frankel. One exercise Hank does is designed to develop his back muscles. He anchors his feet and extends his upper body over the edge of the bench, hands behind his head, shoulders held high.

Hank also does "the Harvard step test." He steps up, alternating legs, to a twenty-inch high bench, then steps down. He repeats the step up, step down, working each leg, until the prescribed number of times is reached. It took some sweat to work up to his maximum number.

Hank's program was carefully designed, as were all others for cardiac patients who were in the original program.

Writing on such exercise plans for the cardiac victim, Dr. Lawrence E. Lamb of Baylor University College of Medicine said in the *Journal of the American Medical Association*, "Like digitalis and most drugs, exercise is useful if prescribed properly." He added that despite the apparent danger of doing *improper* exercises, "the evidence that *proper* exercise programs are beneficial to the heart and circulation is overwhelming."

And to that end Hank Goodall says "Amen."

"I didn't retire immediately from my work after my attack," Hank said. "Hell, I had to eat. I had years to go. I was back at work two months later, only I had a different outlook. For one thing I was slimmer, college weight again—almost. I'd dropped forty pounds. For another I'd learned to appreciate how important each day was and how much I had to live for."

Hank's business office was located on the fifth floor. He used the stairs now to get to it instead of the elevator.

"I also made sure I didn't stay in my office for hours on end, sitting, skipping lunch, often just eating junk from a vending machine for energy. I made a point after I returned to work to select a place where I had to walk to get to it. Afterward I detoured a bit going back, reacquainting myself with my city."

Hank's wife, Mary, said the heart attack affected her habits, too.

"I had to learn not to stuff Hank with his favorite high-calorie dishes. I used to think of them as a treat for him; now I know they were poison. We eat so differently now and because we do, I'm slimmer, too."

Hank did retire this year, sold his business. But he didn't quit work. He's now active in many volunteer projects, serving on boards of various charities. He's also a disciple of Preventive Care, because he's seen, talked to, and touched the lives of those who've enrolled. He's now "in their age bracket" and he's telling everyone who will listen to him that it works. He serves on two speakers' bureaus, and is always in demand.

"I tell middle-aged businessmen that I exercised my way back to health. But *telling* them isn't enough. I'm the living proof.

That, they can't argue with. Hell, after I talk about my attack, and my dramatic recovery, I wouldn't have to say another word. But I do. I sure don't want any of them to learn what I've learned about keeping physically fit—the hard way."

And so Hank talks on.

Chapter 7

If Ella Can't Come to Preventive Care, Then Preventive Care Will Come to Her

TO FIND ELLA Gerald, I had to take up jogging. At ninety-two, this nonagenarian was one of Preventive Care's strongest examples of how even an ancient body can be kept fit.

"What lap are you on, Ella?" I kidded as I fell into step with her lively pace.

"Once around our building each day does me nicely," she said. "I'm ready to go inside, now. I woke up my blood."

We walked together into the home for the elderly where Ella lived. Since Frankel and his team had brought Preventive Care there twice a week, Ella made it a personal mission to prove its worth. Not like many of the others, who shuffled through gray days in a drug-induced fog, Ella was physically and mentally alert. And she hated to be patronized.

"Like my outfit?" she asked as we sat together near the fireplace in the main lounge.

"It's really pretty, Ella. But aren't you afraid of attracting 'wolves whistles' with that outfit on?"

Ella took the kidding, laughed. "Listen, the first time I wore this to a Preventive Care class in the lobby I was downright scared. Thought everybody who could see might make fun of me. Too daring, you know? But then that darling Betty Richard came to give us some exercise and she said, 'Don't you dare go change. Shorts under a tennis dress are just what you need to move about. You look just fine.'

Workout time at Preventive Care classes. Nothing much in the way of equipment is needed except for a mat or rug, dumbbells or vegetable cans for weights, and a fourteen-inch broom handle.

"Well, I sure felt better, then. Some around here still snickered, though. Guess they forgot what legs are for."

"Where is everybody?" I asked.

"Too early for most of them. They've got to crank up to even get themselves out of their beds. Takes some a half day for just that. They can come to breakfast or not—lots of them don't."

"Ella, what makes you stick to your exercises so?"

"Well, I feel better as long as I keep moving. And since I started with the Frankel group, I find I don't have to take the medication. Sure, things still hurt. But I sleep good now. And my mind is sharp."

"That I can see, Ella. But what bugs you about this place? You started to tell me once before. . . ."

"Nothing to do. That bothers me here. I keep fit but I can't find anything to channel my new energy into. Why, if I could, I'd move out of here tomorrow. . . ."

"And do what?"

"Keep house for myself. Find a tiny apartment. Talk to people who talk back. Play cards. Drink a bottle of wine with dinner."

"Why can't you do some of those things now, right here?"

Again Ella laughed, not a squeaky old-age cackle but a deep-throated laugh.

"Around here cards are frowned on. So's wine. Had a bottle sent to me once by a relative for my birthday. Didn't open it, though. They—the staff—suggested I give it away.

"But I'm not complaining, not really. It's just that you people gave me a jolt back into life and now I want to use it, somehow. Reading is out; my eyes aren't that good any more. But I know I could be doing something for somebody. Frankel's team coming here twice a week is the highlight of my week. But it's nothing in-between. Trouble is most folks here were too far gone by the time they got here to ever want to change. They seem content to follow routine. But I'm not. Not any more."

Ella's agility was remarkable. When the Frankel team held a class there, they tossed out a six-pound medicine-exercise ball, told each one to throw it back to the leader. After that warmed them up they'd go into neck, shoulder, and arm exercises. Those in wheelchairs had their own special kind of exercises to perform. Ella followed every one of them.

"You know, I did take a little medicine this week for the first time in a long time," Ella admitted to me. "But lately I've felt so good I just don't take it much any more at all."

"What did your doctor say when you visited him?"

"Ten dollars," she snapped.

Ella's never lost her sense of humor. But she's found it increasingly hard to buck administration policy against organized activity. She was pushing for mental, as well as physical, stimulation.

"There is no fun here, no challenge at all. Why I hear on the radio and TV all about these political campaigns all the time. Sure'd like to see some of those fellows come by here and talk to us. I still vote. Take it seriously, too."

She stopped a moment, looked at me. "Why is it when you get old people think you're a child again? I'm an educated woman, a responsible one, too. I hate it when someone pats me on the shoulder or calls me grandma. I'm not their grandma."

I knew why Ella had outlived most of those in her family. Her spirit was made of steel.

"See? See that old lady going by there, now?" I turned to look at a woman, years Ella's junior. She was using a cane to walk, its taps telegraphing her nearness.

"Yes. She looks lively enough," I said.

"She's a sly one. She came here just a few weeks ago and her whole purpose to date has been trying to find out my age."

"Why don't you tell her, Ella?"

"That's no fun. My friend, Marie, and I try to keep it a secret from her. You know it makes the old gal move around. She goes from one room to another to find out. But nobody knows for sure so they don't tell her. It's just a game we play. Sounds silly, doesn't it? But it adds a little spice, you know? And besides look at all that exercise, that walking, she gets just sliding into and out of all those rooms trying to find out about me. We've even got her into the exercise classes now, too. She tries to outdo me every time. Breaks the monotony of a day."

Ella's family is mostly gone, except for a few relatives out of state. Her husband was a prominent lawyer in West Virginia, and his estate assured Ella of a comfortable old age.

"But you know, I got so unsure of myself when I lived in an

apartment that I actually talked *myself* into coming here. Besides I hate to cook. They do give us nice meals here. But there's no freedom of the spirit. Nothing new."

"What about Preventive Care?"

"Oh, that's fine. And lately I've seen more people in our classes than ever before. And the ones who come are better for it. They don't talk medicine and aches and pains all of the time now. But it's only twice a week. What are we supposed to do with the rest of our time?

"I guess it's just too late for most of us here. I'm sure grateful to Mr. Frankel for thinking of us, though. You know I do get out once in awhile, too. When Mr. Frankel put on a Preventive Care program recently, he asked me to come. I had a great time. Showed them all that high step of mine."

Ella also plays the piano, and well.

"Could you play something for me, Ella, now?"

The elfish woman walked over to the piano, sat down, lifted the lid, and flexed her fingers.

"There's nothing wrong with my fingers. Mr. Frankel also gave me some exercises to do for them, and for the wrists. I follow then even in my room. See, no arthritis in these hands!"

I did see two tiny hands painted with blue veins and wrinkled like ancient maps. But she was right. There was no disfiguration, no gnarling. And her nails, I noticed, were tinted a delicate pink.

"That? A nice young girl from some Girl Scout troop or other came here to pay us one of those 'duty' calls, you know. They offered to pretty us up a bit. This one little girl took to me. She wanted to do my nails. Why not? I let her but I didn't like the feeling they all gave me. As though I were the child and they were the adult. We're not children, you know?"

"I know, Ella. Most of us realize that."

"What would you like to hear?"

"Anything, anything at all."

"My husband doted on Chopin. I played a lot just for him. Did you know I studied for awhile at your Cincinnati Conservatory of Music?

"No, Ella, really?"

"Yes, I did. John, my husband, wanted me to while we were up there. That was sure a long time ago. None of my four children ever played a note. Isn't that funny?"

As she talked, her fingers started to play. It was lovely. She halted more than once, but picked it up again. Then she stopped.

"You know, most of those here don't even like to hear me play. I like an audience. John used to just sit down near me, close his eyes, and smile. I knew it brought him pleasure."

A few were coming into the main lobby now. One very cross woman came up near enough for us to hear, then said to her companion, "Why doesn't she shut off that noise?"

Maybe Ella was right. Perhaps it was too late for most of those in this home. But as Mr. Frankel and his team have said, "We must try to enrich all of the elderly's lives, right now. Many of those in homes like Ella's who take part in Preventive Care need less medication, feel better, and seem to get through the day with a little more spirit. That's a start. But we must reach out to more people before they need custodial care. Then more and more of them will never need to surrender their freedom. Not until that last final illness."

Ella was the home's exception. I wanted her to get out of the place, help her and others take better care of themselves. But I knew she wouldn't go. Under that veneer of bravery, there was fear. Ella had been dependent on others for too many years.

Chapter 8

I Always Wanted to Be a Twiggy

BACK TROUBLE, AND the threat of an operation, brought Hope Rigby, college professor, to the Frankel Institute many years before the gym spawned its public, nonprofit foundation program—Preventive Care. Hope came for help in 1962.

"Actually, I'm quite different from most of those in the Preventive Care program now," Hope said. "Many of them never did any kind of physical activity in all of their lives. I did. Swimming was 'my thing,' as the kids say. I played a lot of tennis, too, when I was younger. But after I took on the job as head of our English department at the university, I found less time to do any kind of exercise."

Then, twelve years ago, Hope's back problem, something she'd lived with for many years, became acute, threatened her job at the university. She found she was miserable no matter how or where she sat in the classroom—the pain was almost unbearable. Driving her car became impossible.

"Hope," her doctor told her after a visit to him, "we've tried a lot of things, but your back isn't any better. It's worse. I have a friend here in Charleston who cooperates with doctors when we have patients in need of therapeutic exercise. I'm going to send you to Lawrence Frankel for some planned exercises on a regular basis. If that doesn't help, then I'm afraid we must consider surgery."

Hope took the slip of paper with Frankel's name on it, drove home, fixed dinner, debated whether or not to call. Then finally she dialed the number, reluctantly, feeling depressed and whipped. What good will it do now? she thought.

65

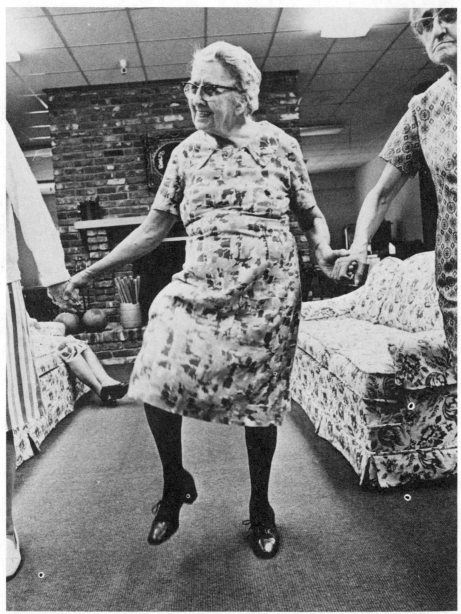

Dancing is not just for the young. Older people enjoy both a lively tune and the companionship of friends. Here an advocate of Preventive Care joins her dance circle in high style, even though she is over eighty years old.

"When I first went to the gym I saw lots of people my own age, and some a lot older, working out. That encouraged me. The gym was like gyms everywhere. The only thing different there was the spirit Frankel injected into those people. Not only did most of them like what they were doing, they felt a real loyalty to this man, real faith in him—and in his programs. I knew he'd dedicated his life to helping people keep physically fit, and knew his stuff, but I just didn't expect all the personal attention."

Hope's program included a three-times-a-week workout.

She also had exercises she was to do at home, all of the time.

"I was determined to follow his plan for me. I didn't have any more options. Besides, I really did like exercise."

After only three weeks in the therapeutic program, Hope found driving her car a pleasure again. Slowly, as she toned up, she found pounds disappearing.

"It was a fluky thing to do," she later told me, "but I felt so good I went in, had my brown hair restyled, changed its color to champagne blonde. I felt like a kid again."

"Sure, some of my college students teased me with that new hair color. I guess they'd always thought of me as an old-maid spinster, all dried up. I shook them up a little."

Hope's story might have ended right there. She was again involved in activities on the campus, expanded her own volunteer hospital work. She was then fifty-three, looked forward to a lot more teaching years because at her university, mandatory retirement didn't come until seventy.

"By then I felt I'd have enough time to work to kill that rule, too. I always thought there should be no set age to retire for anyone. Still do."

But Hope's story didn't end there. She continued for the next twelve years in the physical-fitness program designed for her, enjoying good health. No more back problems.

But the look on her doctor's face after an annual physical checkup last year spelled trouble. She recognized that look.

"What did you find, Doctor?"

"Hope, did you realize you had a small lump on your right breast?"

She didn't. But the doctor felt it was imperative to find out whether or not it was malignant. He ordered her into the hospital immediately. The biopsy was positive. One breast was removed.

"Recovering in the hospital after that major surgery made me do a lot of thinking. At first I thought it was all over, but then I refused to allow that line of reasoning to continue. I wasn't licked—yet."

And it wasn't but a month after Hope left the hospital than she was back in the gym, working out.

Beulah Phillips, Preventive Care's registered nurse who watches over all of those who exercised, looked in on Hope her first day back after the operation.

"I was stunned by her agility, the exercises she was trying to do. I've seen mastectomies who could never lift their arms above their shoulders for months after surgery. And here was Hope, trying. She just wouldn't quit."

But she almost did, a year later, when the doctor said another operation was necessary—to remove the other breast.

"I guess I was feeling really depressed when I entered the hospital that time—sure my life was over. But you know when I woke up I felt quite differently. I was happy to see the sun through my window."

Repeating her prior performance, Hope, now sixty-five, was back at her gymnastic routines, this time determined not only to stay in shape, but to lose even more weight.

"Everyone seemed so shocked that I could return to workout so soon after surgery again. Beulah continued to be amazed. I guess she's seen so many cases like mine that just gave up, she couldn't believe I'd really come back."

It wasn't easy. Everyone could see Hope's struggle in her urgency to return to good health. It went badly at first. But she persisted. Lifting her arms was painful. But she kept at it.

One afternoon late, after most of those working out in the gym had gone, Beulah decided on a sauna. In the bath, too, was Hope.

"You know, Beulah," she told the nurse. "All my life I was kind of pudgy, buxom. I've lost all that extra weight now. And look at me. I'm what I always wanted to be—a real Twiggy, top to toes."

Later, in a more serious mood, Hope discussed with me her

dedication to physical fitness over these past years and her total belief in it now as a life-style.

"Without exercise I'd be dead by now. I know that. First the back, then the double mastectomy. If I'd have quit any one of those times, I'd have withered. I feel so strong now they could cut on me, piece by piece, but like an amoeba, I'd just change my form to fit. Or, make those parts left work better. It's attitude, you know, that keeps us functioning. Mine's positive. And it always will be."

Hope was wearing gray sweat pants and shirt. She looked like a bean stalk. Only five foot, two, she was now down to about 105 pounds, a weight she hadn't enjoyed since high school. She wore her hair styled, but boyish, complementing a deep tan. She liked golfing vacations in the South.

Hope was Preventive Care's personal emissary whenever a new elderly person came into the foundation's program. If she could, she personally talked to each new arrival, encouraging each one of them to try exercise as a way of life. And, finally, to those whose eyes betrayed doubt, she'd say, "By knife or by strife, I won't be defeated. Don't you be. Stay with the program. You'll never be sorry."

"You know," she told me, "I wish every kid in America, from grade school up, had to take physical exercise every day. But not just as a duty. They should be taught its worth and its fun. Then, by the time they were grown, they'd want to continue it all of their lives. I should know. I didn't get back to it until my fifties—almost too late for me, personally. But I sure wouldn't give it up now."

Hope continues to be one of her city's most active hospital volunteers. She regularly visits to cheer up patients. She pushes a "cheer" cart, full of treats, magazines, and books, through the corridors, looking especially for those who have had her kind of medical problems. She wants them to know why her name is—Hope.

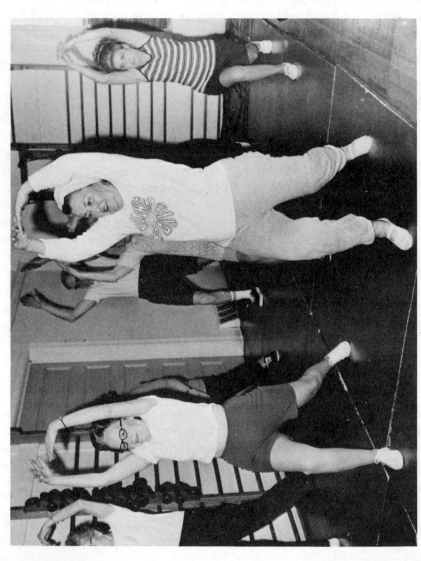

At the Frankel Foundation headquarters in Charleston, West Virginia, classes are held three times a week in Preventive Care. Here a group works on leg lunges.

Chapter 9

"If You Can't Walk, You've Got to Get Out"

CLARA SIDELL KNEW the rules. When she retired from her executive job as director for a large insurance company and moved into the city's newest high-rise apartment building for those sixty-two and older, she signed a lease—and a pledge.

"This apartment is designed for retired persons, sixty-two and older, who are ambulatory. When, in the judgment of the management, the tenant can no longer maintain himself and his apartment, and needs custodial care, the tenant then must surrender his apartment and be moved to full-care facilities."

At sixty-seven, Clara just knew she could manage for many years to come. She had only one problem that bothered her. Her weight. An imposing five foot nine, ramrod straight, Clara distributed those pounds rather well—until recently. Now with time on her hands, she excelled at what she did best in retirement—cooking. Not only for her friends in the building, but for herself. Her weight, usually 176, zoomed to 235 pounds. Then arthritis hit.

"I couldn't walk, bend, or move. They took me to the hospital. There the doctor said, 'Clara, I can't even begin to treat you now. You're in such poor health—and all that weight aggravates your condition. I'm putting you on a strict diet.'"

It was a weak and despondent Clara who returned home from the hospital—helpless. Greeting her were her two closest friends, Fannie and Faye, also residents of the tenth floor. Clara was put to bed immediately, spouting she was unable—and unwilling—to do anything for herself.

71

Aware of the apartment's basic rule of self-help or else, Fannie and Faye mapped out their plan of deception. They agreed they'd feed and serve Clara, take care of her apartment, until she could get back on her feet again. The manager would never know.

"I couldn't even cook for myself. I was always in pain. Soon I didn't even try to get out of bed. My weight soared again, too. I was eating—all of the wrong things—thanks to my two friends who wanted only to help. I got worse and worse."

Then the "move" notice came. Management *had* found out.

Mr. Frankel heard about Clara's plight through a mutual friend, her attorney. It was a desperation call.

"Larry, you've just got to help this woman. She's been issued an ultimatum—either become ambulatory or move out—perhaps to a nursing home."

Frankel and Betty Richard made the first visit to Clara's apartment. She was on the tenth floor. When they arrived, the two elves, Fannie and Faye, who cleaned and cared for Clara were just leaving.

"Clara's in there, in bed. She said you were coming so please just go on in," Faye said.

"Well, hello Clara," Frankel walked into the bedroom with Betty at his side. "Your place is lovely. Quite a view of the city from here. You certainly do like the color blue, don't you?"

"Yes. Only I should have added black to my color scheme because that's what I am—black and blue. Then I'd match."

"Glad to see you in good spirits."

"Good spirits, ha! Do you call lying in bed having to be waited on by two devoted friends good spirits?"

"The question is, Clara, do you want to get out of that bed? Get well?"

"Now there's a question to ask a helpless old woman. Certainly I do. I want to keep breathing, too. But I have no control over that. And I don't have any control over my condition, either."

"But you do. You can make yourself move, if you want to. It will be painful, at first. But you'll have to want to do it more than anything else in your entire life. It's got to be an everyday thing. The exercises I give you must be done every day. No cheating. You'll have to be faithful to the regimen. Or else I can't help you," Frankel said.

"What makes you think I won't?"

"Jim, your attorney. He told me you hate exercise."

"He told you right. I hate it. Never had any need for it. Always was in the best of health before. I really loathe it."

"Well, Clara, if you want to get out of that bed you'll have to change your attitude toward it, From this day on it's exercise—or else."

Clara contorted her face into a look of pure pain.

"Do I have a choice? If I can't find a way to get out of this bed, they'll move me into a nursing home. Then I know I'll die for sure."

"Well?"

"What do you want me to do?"

While Frankel explained the exercises he wanted Clara to start on, Betty demonstrated them. Then together they worked on the first few. They showed her how to exercise her fingers, her wrists, her arms, her legs—even while lying in bed. She was told to practice these and they'd return to check her progress in three days. It was only three weeks until the end of the month, the date management had given Clara to find a solution to her living problem.

When Betty and Lawrence came back three days later, a more cheerful, less bossy Clara greeted them. This time they were able to get her to sit up on the side on her bed. She then was asked to stand, sit, stand, then sit.

At first she balked. "I'll fall."

"Then I'll catch you," Frankel said.

Clara eyed the man whose reputation for strength was legend in Charleston. She'd also heard from Jim about his kindness and the fact that Frankel, like himself in the old days, hated self-pity. She relaxed.

That weekend Clara must have practiced overtime because when Betty came back, alone, to visit the following Tuesday a happy, confident Clara greeted her knock at the apartment door.

"Come on in, the door is open."

Betty found Clara sitting up, at the side of her bed, swinging her feet. She grinned broadly, a really friendly smile.

"You must feel much better?"

"I feel really great today, Betty. I've done everything Mr. Frankel and you asked me to do. Now, I have one big question."

"And that is . . . ."

"When do I start getting to look like you?"

Betty laughed. Her 115-pound well-proportioned figure was the envy of every woman in all Preventive Care classes. Many kidded Betty they'd try anything if she could guarantee that they'd have a figure like hers.

"Clara, you've lost many pounds since you went to the hospital. Why, when we finish with you you'll be a raving beauty."

"I feel that way already. Finally someone cares how *I* feel. You and Mr. Frankel seem like old friends. I couldn't do it without you. I think I want to walk again *just* like you."

"Good. Because today you *are* going to walk."

"Oh. Well. Now, Betty, you know what I meant. Sometime soon—yes. But, God, Betty, not today. It's . . . I'm . . . not ready." Her voice turned cross.

Betty ignored her remarks, her slip into the self-pity routine.

"Today we walk." Betty went over to get the walker Clara's doctor had ordered for her. She pushed it to her bedside.

"Betty, I hate the sight of that thing. Reminds me I'm old."

"Nonsense. Think of it as a friend who's going to help you walk again. We are going to walk to your bathroom and back, together. Then you are going to do it solo."

"Betty, I couldn't."

"Clara, you must."

Together they started the first of several walks to the bathroom, Betty, Clara, and the walker—all of twelve feet away. At first Clara, who dwarfed Betty, faltered, and threatened to stop. But Betty guided her into a confident performance.

"Now, we'll take one more giant step, to view the city from your living-room picture window."

They made it. Then back again to the bed.

"When is Mr. Frankel coming back into town?" an excited Clara asked when Betty settled her down for a rest.

"He'll return next Monday."

When Mr. Frankel rang Clara's doorbell on Monday with Betty at his side, Clara called out, "It's unlocked. Come in, you two." She was up and waiting for them, seated in a chair near her bed, her walker at her side. She smiled ear to ear. What she didn't know was, this was graduation day.

Frankel and Betty crossed over to her side. "Today Clara, you are going to take a walk with me, arm in arm," Frankel said. "We will go outside of your apartment, up and down this "tenth" floor, and maybe long enough at your friends' apartment to thank Faye and Fannie for the fine job they've done taking care of you. And that they no longer have to."

She gaped at Frankel in astonishment. "No, Mr. Frankel. No. I couldn't. I'm not ready. These legs aren't ready. Didn't Betty tell you I've been using the walker? I can't do it alone."

The speech sounded rehearsed as if Clara had it prepared in case he should issue a command performance.

Betty went to Clara's closet, selected a colorful robe, and brought it to her, along with her slippers. "We're ready, Clara."

"You'll be fine. Now please stand up," Frankel said.

Clara got out of her chair. She knew if she didn't the team was through with her.

Kindly Mr. Frankel said, "Here, Clara, take my arm. It's a beautiful day. You owe yourself a walk."

She faltered. "I'll fall. I know I'll fall."

"Nonsense," Betty assured her. "We're right here with you."

Clara did try to retreat to her chair once but Frankel's grip prevented that. Betty stayed on one side of her, Frankel on the other. Clara took her first steps.

"Now, Betty, suppose you get the front door so Clara and I can take our walk and stop to see her friends."

Together, Clara, who was nearly Frankel's height, and Frankel, walked slowly up and down the hall. With each step she grew more confident.

"It's like being a child again, learning how to walk for the first time," Clara said, thrilled with her own performance.

Then—silence. The walk continued. Both knew now the transformation "took." Clara was well. Gone was the crippled old lady. In her place had metamorphosed a well, confident woman who could now take care of herself.

Two weeks after Frankel had started therapeutic exercises for Clara, she was well enough to come downstairs to the apartment's lobby to watch the Preventive Care's program in action. The participants were residents and those from the surrounding neighborhoods.

But Clara was indignant at what she saw.

"I can't believe out of more than two-hundred people who live here that there are so few in this class. It should be standing room only," she told Frankel.

There were only eighteen attending class that day, the majority of whom had come from outside the building.

"Where are all the people who live here?"

Frankel calmed Clara and reminded her of a woman he once knew who hated exercise of any kind and said "Who needs it?"

"Okay. So rub it in. You're right, of course. But I know *now* what it can mean. They'll end up like I was. Maybe they won't even get that second chance."

"Suppose you tell them that," Frankel challenged.

And Clara did. She's knocked on doors in that apartment house every day, a few at a time, inviting herself in, then pitching her story to them. She said she wouldn't quit until she'd seen everyone there at least once.

When I talked to Clara last, I asked her how she'd motivated those to come down and try exercises, or even learn regimens they could do, alone, in their rooms.

"All they have to do is look at me. I'm their answer. I tell them I'd be in a nursing home if it wasn't for Preventive Care. Instead I'm starting a new business. I'm a representative for a clearing house here to sell magazine subscriptions to large institutions. My own business, and all done on the telephone. I've started living again—and cooking less.

"You know," she added, "some people die at thirty, but aren't buried until sixty. They aren't living. I ask them, 'Say, how old were *you*—when you died?'"

"Clara, you're a devil. There's no stopping you now," I told her.

Chapter 10

"Mom Did All She Could as Long as She Could"

THE QUILT WAS larger than the quorum. Sewing up a storm were five elderly women, "regulars" who met in the apartment house's recreation room just off the lobby three days a week. They could stitch as rapidly as they could talk.

"Making patch quilts is interesting, girls," Myrtle Bloom told them. "But I say we should try something new. What can we lose but an afternoon away from sewing?"

All of the women were over sixty-five. Myrtle, at seventy-five, was their leader. They looked up, listened to her, but went right on with their work. They were used to Myrtle talking, and jumping up and down, and fetching coffee and soft drinks for the others. To their dismay, she'd often bounce off whenever she saw someone she knew getting off the elevator to personally greet them.

That day the seamstresses were alone in the rec room. Not even the mammoth television set was in use.

Myrtle came back from still another work stoppage, ready to present her final arguments on Preventive Care. Elizabeth, who knew a lot about needling as well as needles, eyed Myrtle's slight frame, and said, "*You* exercise, Myrtle? Why you'd just blow away."

"Besides," Annette joined in, "who needs exercise? I get enough of that, yawning."

The rest giggled. But Myrtle wasn't easily defeated.

"Don't you see? We could be doing something that might make us feel real good. After sewing session I actually hear my bones age."

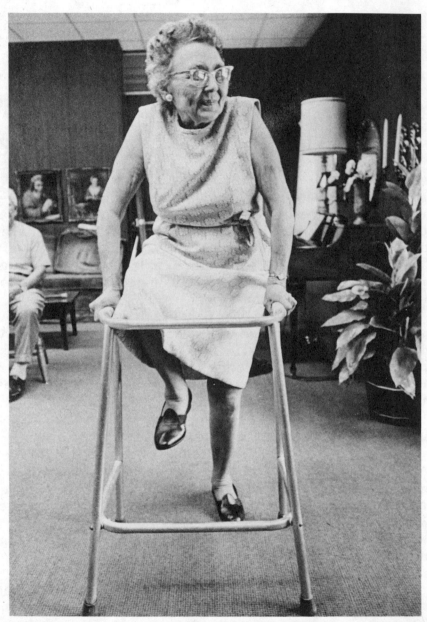

Handicapped persons are not forgotten in the Preventive Care exercises. Those who must use a walker can follow a prescribed routine, too.

Myrtle won. The five agreed to attend the next Monday session at Preventive Care's headquarters just five blocks away from their own apartment building.

"But how will we get there?" Patricia asked. "We have no transportation."

Myrtle eyed Patricia's girth. "Walk," she said.

They lost Patricia after the second class. Then Annette, too. But three remained loyal to the program—Myrtle, Mary and Henrietta.

Each Monday, Wednesday, and Friday, they would meet in the lobby of their apartment building, walk to the Frankel Foundation and participate in exercises to strengthen their heart, lungs, and muscles. Each carried to class a small bag for their gym clothes.

The day we caught up with Myrtle she had just changed from her workout clothes back into a flaming-red wool dress. Her hair was professionally set in a smart, short style. The only "big" thing about Myrtle was her shaggy black eyebrows that shaded snapping black eyes. The eyebrows looked stitched on like a last-minute thought. She stared at me, unbelieving that anyone would want to interview *her.*

"I haven't done anything," she replied in modesty to my questions. "I'm seventy-five, sure, but I'm not the oldest one here. I love doing the exercises, though. And I love coming here with my friends and meeting new people."

Myrtle's been in the program now for two full years. "I had a bad spell, though, one time. I was sitting on my couch in my apartment getting ready to come to a Wednesday class when it hit me. The worst pain up my back I'd ever had.

"The next thing I knew I was in a hospital."

They put Myrtle in traction. Diagnosis—severe arthritis. Pain pills eased the attack.

"What did I think of while I was lying there? You'd never guess. I was praying my new doctor wouldn't take away my exercise classes from me when I got out."

At first Myrtle couldn't move much. But she did try to wiggle her hands and feet, whenever she could. The new doctor arrived one morning to find her busy talking to her big toe.

"What are you doing, Myrtle?"

"I'm exercising. My toes don't want to work but after I get

through lashing them some they'll respond. Have to." Myrtle hesi-itated a minute then took a deep breath. She'd rehearsed this question so often.

"Doctor, you just *can't* take away my exercises from me. You wouldn't do that, would you? They mean so much to me. Just go-ing to a class. . . ."

"Easy, Myrtle. I haven't done anything, yet. I know about your classes. When you, and your toes, are ready to walk back to class, I'm ready."

"Oh, Doctor, that's the best news I've had since you strapped me into this contraption. Now just watch me mend."

And she did. A week after she was out of the hospital Myrtle was on the phone to Henrietta, announcing the time had come for them to resume their walks to the Frankel Foundation head-quarters.

"We were so afraid you'd never be able to come to class any more," Mary told Myrtle as they started out of the lobby that cold November morning. "It's not much fun without you."

Thinking back now to that hospital stay and the recovery, Myr-tle confided, "It wasn't easy coming back. I hurt—lots. But after I warmed up a bit, I found it all coming back to me. I like the leg lunges best because I think they do the most for me." She stood up in Frankel's crowded office, pushed aside a chair, and demon-strated.

"You see, you thrust forward on one leg, hold, and then return to closed standing position. Then you do that with the other leg. They help me the most. And you know, I never had to take any pain pills or sleeping pills since I started back to exercising again. I'm able to sleep right off now."

Myrtle's offspring, including three girls, two boys, thirteen grandchildren, and two great-grandchildren, hold her in awe. They've seen Grandma Bloom perform on television in a Preven-tive Care demonstration group, and at other civic gatherings.

"I went to Texas to visit my eighteen-year-old grandson for a few days," Myrtle told me. "That scamp was making fun of me when I demonstrated the exercise routine I followed. He told me, 'Granny, those are old-ladies' exercises.' "

Myrtle then went into high gear. She demonstrated her endurance exercises, including straddles, strides, run in place, hop on each foot, etc., lasting about two minutes. She invited him to join her. He quit before the timer went off.

" 'Granny, I apologize,' he told me," Myrtle said as she winked a wicked black eye, . . . *after* he'd caught his breath.

"You know, I raised five children and never did any kind of exercise like this before. Sure, I kept house and that was work, plenty of it. But I never really took the time to do anything for myself to make *me* feel better.

"Now I do the Preventive Care exercises and love them. I really like to demonstrate them to others, too. My kids, grandchildren, and friends, are proud of me, I think."

Myrtle claims she has two missions left. One is to blast her middle-aged children into doing exercise *now*, before they get old, and the other is to make her grandchildren and great-grand-children aware of the role exercise plays in a successful life-style.

"I didn't start out to try to change anybody else except my sewing friends," Myrtle said, "but now I can't help myself. I want everyone I know to share the great feeling I have now. Sure, I still have pain but I don't mind that. I've got kidney problems, too, but that don't bother me none. I'm not even thinking about it and because the pains don't get my attention, they don't take over. I do."

Myrtle hasn't quit her quilt making. She still does that as part of the talkative fivesome. She also is into making costume jewelry and ceramics.

"The new handicrafts aren't just busy work. We have a little room over there," she pointed to the room just off the front door of the lobby, "where we've opened a little gift and thrift shop four days a week. Anything we want to sell goes in there. I've realized more than pocket change from my sales. There's so many designs I have in mind now. It's a whole new thing for me."

Myrtle still attends her childhood church way across town every Sunday. "My family picks me up each week so we always get a chance to see each other."

Myrtle chuckled to herself. "Not all the missionary work goes on inside my church. I met a lady there last week and convinced her to try Preventive Care's program. She came this week for the first time. So, you see, I'm bringing in 'converts.' "

"But Myrtle," we asked, "if you had to do these exercises alone, say in your apartment, would you keep them up?"

"Maybe not," she admitted, "can't say. I'm used to them and I'd miss them. But you need a lot of self-discipline to stay with them alone, regularly. I think if I wasn't in a class, and I couldn't go to the foundation any more, *I'd* form my own group. I like being with others."

"And what about the others who live here in the apartment? How can Preventive Care reach them?"

"Can't. Not some at least. They sit so close to their television, it's a wonder it doesn't swallow them whole. But if their doctors said, 'Exercise or else,' I think they'd listen. I tell as many as I can about my hospital stay and the pain that hurt so bad it seemed they'd taken a saw and cut my leg clear off. But they just smile or say, 'Shh, Jane here on TV is about to run away with Linda's husband,' and turn back to their soap opera.

"You know what I wish? I wish I could be inside that television set just once, bounce a stick off their toes, and make them dance a jig. Then after they did I'd say, 'You can dance. See? How about joining us?' "

Myrtle's high-octane energy reflects itself in her apartment, too. She brought with her from her own large home several pieces of polished Early American furniture and lots of green plants.

"I've got a green thumb, they tell me. There's nothing that doesn't grow for me 'cause I talk to my plants. Scientists now say that works. I knew that years before they did."

Did she ever think about the tomorrows when some of her energy might dissipate?

"Of course, You can't go on forever. But I'm going to for as long as I can be independent. Then my children can say of me, 'Mom did all she could as long as she could.' That's not a bad way of ending, is it?"

Chapter 11

June Taylor Dancers, Here Comes Pat

THE ONLY EXERCISE Pat Arnette ever did was push the button for an elevator and flip the switch to turn on her washing machine and dryer.

"Really, that's the truth," the seventy-two year-old "dancing star" told me.

"Exercise, ugh. That's for kids. At least that's what I thought."

Pat changed her mind. But it took widowhood, two broken legs, months wallowing in self-pity and lethargy, to bring about a change.

After her husband's death, Pat found life untenable. She couldn't keep her mind on anything. In that comatose state she crashed her late-model car into the rear end of another car while driving home on a highway interchange. The crash left her with lifeless legs.

"You may never walk again," they told Pat. But her doctor urged her to be patient.

She was. She embraced patience. She used it as her excuse to quit. She told herself, when her legs wouldn't respond, that time heals all things, even this. And because time was on her side she accepted her wheelchair as a friend, never once trying to fight its possession of her.

Like other widows who find themselves suddenly alone, and afraid, Pat found it much easier to accept her handicap than try to correct it.

A deep depression followed. Forced to sell her home, Pat sought

83

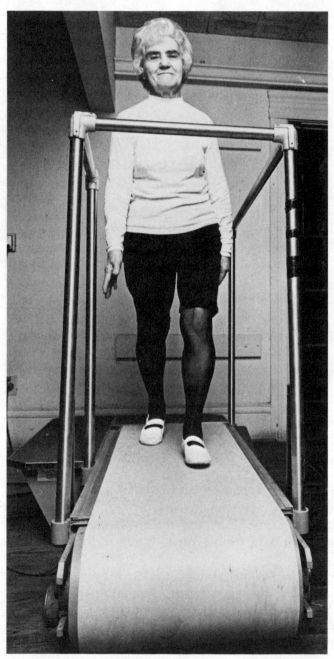

One of the pieces of equipment used for Preventive Care enrollees who regularly visit the Frankel Foundation's gymnasium in Charleston, West Virginia, is the treadmill. Some put as much as six miles of walking on it in a day.

"shelter" from the world in a residence institution where custodial care was offered. She even depended on her wheelchair for her infrequent visits to the main lobby, even though in her room she found her legs were able to hold her weight now, didn't seem as stiff. She didn't have any reason to try, because there was no one to care whether she walked or not. A sense of futility followed.

For months after her move to the home, Pat did nothing for herself. She read, watched television, stared at the others. They stared back. No one offered friendship. She went further into limbo.

Then one afternoon Pat caught a public service announcement on television about the Frankel Foundation's new program for those over sixty-five. Several older people demonstrated their agility. Pat caught the phrase, "You in wheelchairs can be helped, too."

Why not? she thought. I haven't been out of this place in a long time.

The next day Pat dialed the foundation number three times, and for three times, after it rang, she hung up. You old fool, she told herself, what makes you think you can get help from total strangers? Do you think they can perform miracles? Your legs are useless. And besides, who cares?

When she finally stopped chastising herself, she dialed the number and let it ring. The voice that answered assured her, "We care. Get your doctor's permission and come to class whenever you are ready."

That wasn't right away. Pat decided to try walking again, in her room, with crutches. Her legs were stiff and it hurt. But after many sessions she felt confident enough to call a cab, and hobble over to the foundation—for what, she wasn't sure.

She started the exercises in slow motion. Mr. Frankel gave her special routines just for her legs, and to wake up her circulation. It went slowly. The low-mobility patterns were designed to strengthen her legs, and give her a sense of accomplishment. Each time she visited the foundation class, she found strength to do still more.

About five months after Pat had started her exercise back to health, she walked into the gym using just her own two legs.

"Fine," Mr. Frankel and Betty told her. "Now let's see you dance."

Pat thought they were insane. But she loved the music that played during the hour-long class and often found herself tapping out the rhythm with her foot. She looked at Betty, and then at Lawrence Frankel, and knew she had to at least try. They wanted her to so badly. They cared. She joined the dance circle that formed at the closing of each session and tried to do some of the steps.

"I felt like size-nine shoes squeezed into size-four slippers. Clumsy and awkward. And hurting. But it was kind of fun."

After that Pat joined the finale of every class, each time with a little more agility in the dance routine.

It wasn't long before she was bringing to class a few dance patterns of her own for the rest to try. And she told them of her plans to move out of the full-care facility where she lived.

"Where will you go?" Betty asked her after a class workout.

"I've got a job. Would you believe that? I've got a job. I'm a really good cook, you see, and one of the women from the class told me about a school cafeteria that needed help. I applied and got it. Now I'm going to move into an apartment and care for myself again. I know I can."

Pat did return to work. She also returned to be one of the leaders in the Preventive Care classes. Her dance routines were fun for everyone.

"When I first started into these classes, I don't think dancing ever entered my mind. The thing I related to most was the medicine ball, what Mr. Frankel calls the 'hostility release.' I know it was for me. I'd toss that six-pound ball to the next person in line with a vengeance. I didn't realize at the time that I was also exercising my arms. All I could think of was, 'There, you so-and-so. Take that.'"

Later on Pat realized she was breaking down the barriers she, herself, had set up against relationships with other people. Her anger at her accident had estranged her from any companionship she might otherwise have had.

And dance? "I've gone beyond that Preventive Care class now. I went to a senior group meeting here in the city and found some other people there who had lots in common with me. I'm now in a folk-dance club and I love it. Why, at the rate I'm going, I may end up as a June Taylor dancer on TV."

Chapter 12

We've Got a Date

IT WAS ALMOST closing time at the Frankel Foundation. Lawrence, as usual, was one of the last ones to leave the place. His 70-75-hour week found him greeting the morning people who came to work out and saying goodby to the evening ones.

Lawrence could hear the shower going upstairs, near his office. He went down to check out the first floor, found one man still walking miles in place on the treadmill. He had planned to meet his wife, Dorothy, for dinner in half an hour, so he went back up to his office, made a few notes, then prepared to leave. Just as he put on his coat, he heard a soft tap at his office door. He opened it to find, not the night cleaning crew, but Mrs. Sue Lytle, one of the members in the private club that shared "housing" with the foundation.

"I thought almost everyone but a few of the men had gone."

"No, Lawrence, I'm running late, too. I wanted a sauna before I left and besides, I really wanted to stay long enough to find you free for a moment to talk."

Lawrence asked her in, took off his coat, and motioned her to sit down.

"I came begging a favor, Lawrence." Sue told him. "It's my mother-in-law. Her name is Mrs. Lee Petersen. She's ninety-two and needs special help—your kind of help."

"Why? Has she a physical problem?"

"No, actually she's quite all right—for an old lady. She did, however, take a fall last week, and was rushed off to the hospital for

Lawrence Frankel often joins his Preventive Care classes to dance with friends. Here a "young" woman of eighty-five is all smiles as she steps into a routine of her youth.

x-ray. They found nothing broken. It shook her up quite a bit, though. Now she's in a wheelchair for the first time in her life. She hates it. But she says her legs won't support her any more. The doctor thinks she's just afraid of falling again."

"What do you want *me* to do, Sue?"

"If you could, visit with her and see if you can help her get out of her wheelchair. I have talked with our doctor and obtained his written consent for you to work with her on exercises for her legs—if she's willing. She's such a bright old gal, you know. A great conversationalist. Help her if you can. She has such dignity and pride. We all love her so."

Frankel promised Sue he'd try to visit Mrs. Petersen within a few days. He checked his schedule, found it tight with classes, lectures, individual programs. But there was always lunch.

That Tuesday, Lawrence, who watches his weight to keep it near the two-hundred-pound mark, decided he needed only a light lunch that day, thus affording him time to talk to Mrs. Peterson. To find a ninety-two-year-old who hated her wheelchair and wanted out would be refreshing.

A practical nurse let Lawrence into the Peterson home. Fifteen minutes later, Lawrence and Lee were talking together like old friends. Lee, who for years taught and supervised in public-school classrooms in the county, was a fighter. And a reader. She had stacks of paperbacks near her side, and a medical dictionary handy.

"I know what I've got and what they think I've got," she told Frankel. "I've always had this touch of arthritis and they think I'm using that as an excuse not to get up and walk. My wheelchair addiction is psychosomatic, they think. I agree. But no one has told my legs that."

Lawrence listened while Lee explained about her fall and the "weakness" that followed. He also knew that if Lee didn't exercise those legs immediately, her chances of getting out of that wheelchair were nil. He remained silent for a minute. Then he put his arms on either side of Lee's wheelchair, looked her straight in the eye and said, "You and I have a date—to walk."

Lee, who'd stared down man and boy in classrooms for more than fifty years, didn't even blink. Instead she said, "A date? What for? I never date younger men."

They both laughed.

"Well," Frankel continued, "It's now January. In March, we—you and I—are going to promenade around this house just like you did before your accident. You are going to take steps on your own and be master again over those reluctant legs. That's going to make you independent again. *That's* our date."

"Quite a tall order for an old lady who can't even get up off her fanny."

"You can. And you will. I promise. Besides, I've never been turned down for a date before and I don't intend to start now."

They kept teasing and exchanging barbs each time they met, which usually was on Tuesday and Thursdays during Lawrence's brief lunch hour away from his classes and lecture committments. Each time Lawrence came he worked with Lee, who had her practical nurse at her side, went over old exercises, then presented new ones for her to master. Each time Lee had to do warm-up routines for her arms and fingers. Then the regimens would get slightly harder, increasing the circulation flow throughout her system. The only part of Lee that didn't need stimulation was her mind. Her wit was finely honed.

"How much time do we have before that big date?" she'd ask.

"Well, Lee, I've been coming here now for a month. We've got February and three weeks in March. The last Saturday in March is our walking date."

"Whatever does your wife say, devoting all your spare time to me?"

"She loves it. She rooting for you, too."

Lee's laughter delighted all of them, the practical nurse, Frankel, and Lee's poodle dog, who somehow knew his mistress was feeling better.

"You two seem to be having such a good time I'll just slip out and start lunch while you go through the exercises once again," the nurse said.

"Wait," Lawrence told her, "today I want you to watch the entire session."

The nurse sensed something special about the way he said that and didn't resist his plea.

"Watch us," Lawrence said.

First he had Lee stand up in front of her wheelchair, then sit down, then stand up, then sit down. Twenty times. Then he walked the length of the room, about twenty feet, and brought back with him Lee's metal walker.

"Lawrence, I can't walk, not even with that thing," Lee was already protesting. "Nurse here and I tried but this one leg won't budge."

"We'll try it together," he said.

"Why? Won't do any good."

"Because I want you to."

"Never could refuse a person when he is so polite. Let's go."

Lee stood up, gripped her hands around the rail of the walker. With Lawrence at her side, she pushed it ahead of her, threw out the right leg, then stopped.

"The other one is stuck, Lawrence."

The nurse, on a signal from Lawrence, lifted her left leg and put it in front of her right.

"Now back to the right leg," Lawrence said. Each step was executed with Lee taking the first one, the nurse lifting her bad leg and extending it up ahead. Slowly they crossed the room. Then Lee stopped.

"I can't turn around in this fool contraption, you know."

Lawrence pulled up a side chair, put it behind her, and turned Lee around. "Sit in the chair now. Then we'll walk back."

"I can't go on any further."

"Did you accept 'can't' from your students in all those years in schools?" Lawrence challenged her. "All your life was dedicated to helping others learn. Now it's time to teach yourself—to walk."

Lee didn't need any further prodding. She was going to try. Before they were halfway to home base and the wheelchair, she was moving both legs, even though the bad one dragged.

"You made it!" the nurse shouted, as they seated Lee in the wheelchair.

"Yes, I did," Lee replied, "if you can count two strong arms on your right side holding you, and two strong hands on your left side moving your leg for you."

"Now, Lee . . ." Frankel interrupted.

"I know. I know. It's progress. But I'm sure going to look funny walking every place with a nurse attached to my left leg."

For ten weeks Frankel continued to bring his therapeutic exercises to Mrs. Lee Petersen. Each time he'd visit, Lee would have read still another paperback book and was ready to digest it for him. She pointed to the newest one, open flat on the desk near her wheelchair.

"That book really 'tells it like it is' as the kids say. It's a book about *real* Indians, not at all that Hollywood nonsense. You know, I never realized how many Indians there were in this country before we came here. I don't know why I didn't. I just never really cared, I guess. Now I do. At ninety-two I do care, deeply. I wish there were some way to undo the wrong we've done to these people."

Lawrence often would just listen to Lee review her books, and commented only when he'd read one of them she had, or read a new one he thought she'd be interested in. He knew these book chats further stimulated Lee, kept her alert and receptive to new ideas—including walking again. Beside, he himself was an insatiable reader and thoroughly enjoyed the talks.

The "walker" walks were coming along better now. Smoother. Lee dismissed her nurse's pair of hands, but looked to Lawrence for both physical and mental support while she used her walker, or "chariot," as she called it.

"I do feel so much better. I think I *will* be able to walk for our date—with my chariot along."

"No. No way. I like my dates to walk holding on to my arm, not a walker. Maybe we can even dance a little, too."

"What! Dance? Like you do in those classes? Why, you're teasing me."

"No. I'm serious."

Lee sighed. "Do you really think I could? Will I keep that date?"

"I know it"

"Fine. Then what kind of corsage do I get?"

Larry broke into laughter. He promised something special.

The second week in March, Lee took a few steps without the walker but with Lawrence holding her on one side, the nurse on the other.

Just that morning the nurse told Lee, "It won't be long, Mrs. Petersen, and you'll be back into your old routine of caring for yourself. Then your housekeeper Sally will only have to come in for breakfast and lunch. You'll be well enough to make dinner yourself, just like before."

"There's only one thing I'm thinking of now—that walking date," said the petite educator.

Frankel showed up the last day in March for the big date. The nurse let him in. In his hands was a white box, tied with blue ribbon.

"You got my corsage?" Lee called out from the living room.

"Wouldn't have come without it," Frankel said.

Lee was sitting on her couch, dressed in a pale-blue cotton dress, with matching shoes. She wore her abundant white hair puffed up high, brushed into curls.

"Nurse here fixed up my hair. Fooled around with it like I was a schoolgirl going to her first prom. I don't know why. I'm not going to budge."

Lawrence exchanged surprise looks with the nurse.

"What's this? Not going anywhere? Nonsense. You're dressed and ready for a special occasion. Here, look at your flowers."

Lee opened the box, stared at the tinted blue flowers, and sighed.

"The nurse told you I was wearing blue. I can't keep any secrets around here." Lee was obviously pleased. "Well, might as well get up and try. Can't waste this pretty new outfit or these flowers."

The nurse started for Lee. Frankel motioned her to stop. Instead he offered Lee his arm. She stood up.

"Lawrence I . . . ."

"Let's walk."

"Don't you see, I'm too . . . ."

"Walk."

Lee took her first halting steps. Then she grew a little more confident. However, she nodded to her nurse, saying, "Do stay close by. I want to be sure."

The two of them, Frankel and Lee, walked the length of her living room, rested, and then went into the entry hall, the kitchen and back. It was slow, difficult work for Lee. But she kept at it.

"Lawrence, do you treat all of your dates so mean?" Lee teased. She sat down heavily into her favorite chair. "I haven't worked so hard in years."

But her face was radiant. She had walked. She'd taken those first steps on her own power just as Frankel had promised she would when they first met weeks ago. Her doctor had warned her that unless she used her legs, they would be permanently impaired. Now that crisis had passed.

"If you hadn't of walked today for me, Lee," Frankel told her, "I might have had to eat my words. That's not my idea of appetizing fare. From here on in, all you need to do is practice with your nurse until you feel confident enough to walk without her. You're the master now. Your legs again are yours to obey *your* commands."

Lee grasped his hand. "Lawrence, I'm a grateful old woman. I'll miss you. But I'm not afraid to try now. You've given me back my will." She looked down at her legs, flexed her ankles, and stared at her new shoes.

"You know, today gave me a double treat. I walked alone for the first time and had an excuse to buy a pretty new outfit, too. And date a younger man." She winked. "And like they say in those Westerns, I read, Lawrence, you're a man who really walks tall."

Chapter 13

Support for Preventive Care

"I SINCERELY BELIEVE that it is Nature's plan that we remain physically and mentally alert to the end of our days," said Dr. Dwight H. Murray, a past president of the American Medical Association.

Our legislators think so, too. West Virginian Senator Jennings Randolph was so impressed with the initial program of Preventicare that he recorded his remarks about it in the Congressional Record. His hope—that Preventive Care will engulf the nation, sweeping in a new way of life for Americans.

So, on December 29, 1970, Senator Randolph reported: "Such a program (Preventive Care) is worthy of our careful attention—if the goals of the project are met, then it could well be the model for a nationwide physical fitness plan for older Americans.

"These individuals, who range in age from sixty-five to ninety-two, were either suffering from chronic conditions or recovering from acute physical disabilities—conditions which had rendered them almost completely immobile. But that was before they began participating in a program of physical fitness for the 'Senior Citizens' developed by the Lawrence Frankel Foundation, and funded by a Title III Older Americans grant from the West Virginia Commission on Aging.

"Only six months after beginning a series of carefully supervised, individualized calisthenics classes they are able to participate in community activities and social contacts instead of watching from the sidelines in loneliness and depression, as was the case for many of them previously."

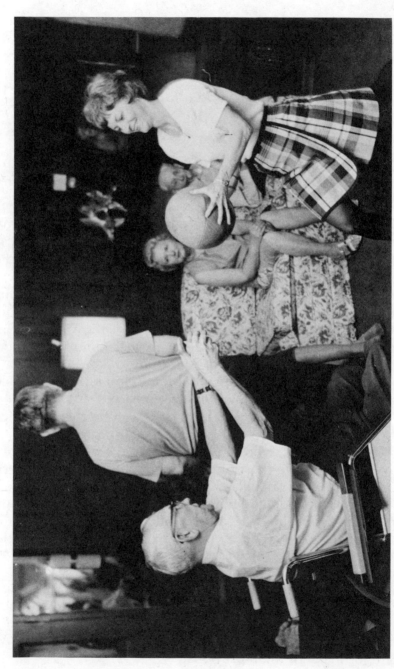

Even those confined to a wheelchair can do Preventive Care exercises. Betty Richard, instructor for the program, tosses a six-pound medicine ball to residents of a retirement home. Many call it their "hostility ball" because it allows them to release bottled up tensions.

Illinois Senator Charles H. Percy also is in accord with Randolph's hope that Preventive Care's concept will go national. He wrote Frankel: "I am a firm believer in the value of carefully planned physical-fitness programs as a means of not only improving one's health but one's general outlook on life as well. Your efforts to mitigate the debilitating effects of habitual physical inactivity among the aged seem most worthwhile, and I hope you will continue your good work."

More and more medical men and specialists feel the same way. On March 1-3, 1973, in Charleston, Frankel called the First Appalachian Conference on Aging, co-sponsored by the Kanawha Valley Heart Association and the Kanawha Medical Society. He brought to his city famous men from all over the world to share their knowledge and views on aging. They all left convinced of one thing—physical activity, as practiced in Preventive Care programs, does slow aging. They not only heard it, they saw it. For, on the stage during the three-day conference, Frankel's groups of aging Americans went through their vigorous exercise regimen. They excited everyone who viewed them.

The "students" who performed for the visiting medical authorities put on demonstrations about an hour in length, always with soft music in the background. They told everyone who would listen they indeed had found a new life-style.

At informal gatherings later on in the confab, Dr. Hans Kraus told Frankel and Betty Richard, "I think your plan is excellent and well formulated. It is indeed one that is very much needed."

Dr. Raymond Harris who heads the Subdepartment of Cardiovascular Medicine at St. Peter's Hospital and is assistant professor of medicine at Albany Medical College, in Albany, New York, went one step further. He told Preventive Care's board of directors: "If you get your project off the ground, I think it should add much necessary information about physical exercise for the elderly. In my opinion, appropriate physical exercise is one of the best ways of improving the health of older people . . . I am in whole accord with your project."

Dr. Daniel Brunner, head of the University of Tel Aviv's Department of Physiological Hygiene in Israel, was enthusiastic, too. Brunner was the doctor dramatized by author Leon Uris in his novel *Exodus*. It was Brunner who organized and carried endangered children from an Israeli kibbutz across a mountain pass through enemy territory to safety.

An advocate of Preventive Care, Dr. Brunner invited Frankel and his team to attend the International Conference on Gerontology in Israel in 1975.

Meanwhile, he told Frankel: "I will try to bring Preventive Care's programs to my people now. I was most impressed with the mental and psychological effects of exercise on your elderly of Charleston. They were so much more alert mentally than others their age who do nothing. We must learn to give life to our years, not just years to our life."

The main thought that all the doctors who attended the First Appalachian Conference took home with them was summarized by Dr. Harris who said: "I, as a doctor, am going to have to learn to prescribe exercise to my older patients—all doctors must. Then we must see to it that programs such as Preventive Care here are supervised by trained individuals. Then it should be implemented everywhere in this country—and later abroad."

Dr. Herbert deVries of UCLA added that perhaps "We should not wait until people are sixty, seventy, and eighty to urge exercise as a life-style. We should find ways to excite young people to participate, too."

Dr. Ernst Jokl, who has been active in research on aging and exercise for more than twenty years, said Preventive Care offers an individual "human values." He explained that programs such as this defy the tyranny of data, and that we know that those who apply Preventicare find—it works.

Dr. Harris did caution, however, that "People won't exercise unless they think this is really what they *want* to do. So now it's up to us, all of us, to tell them this *is* what they want to do."

But how? Most of us agree exercise is good for us. It's like saying, brush your teeth twice a day and see your dentist twice a year. Nice phrases but they don't "get you" where you live. There is an old adage that goes, "Recession is when your neighbor gets fired; depression is when you do." *that's* when it's felt. We must make the *need* for exercise "touch us" just as personally. We must want it as badly as a new color-television set. Just as not eating will starve our bodies, not exercising will make them rust. We've got to be convinced that we cannot live another day without exercising.

One bit of research should help us all. It comes from Dr. Alexander Leaf, a Jackson professor of clinical medicine, Harvard Medical School, and Chief of Medical Services at Massachusetts General Hospital, Boston.

Dr. Leaf has long been intrigued with longevity when it produces men and women who can remain in vigorous health and retain their mental capacities to age one hundred or longer.

To research these people over one hundred and find out why they live so long, Dr. Leaf went to three places around the globe where old age is taken for granted. His mission was to find out why this is so.

In "Three Score and Forty," published in the *Intellectual Digest* of March, 1974, Dr. Leaf reported on the three places he had studied: Vilcabamba, in the Andean mountain terrain of Ecuador; a district called Abkhazia in the Caucasus Mountains of the USSR; and the province of Hunza in the Karakoram Mountains, a part of Pakistani-controlled Kashmir.

He visited Vilcabamba first, where he found that its centenarians are of mixed genetic origins, which told him that "no single genetic factor was involved in their longevity." That meant that you and I, even though our parents are of mixed stock, won't be banned from the exclusive circle of long-life "possibles" on the basis of our heritage alone. Genetics are not a major factor.

Dr. Leaf then studied the diets of these three communities. In Vilcabamba the old people are almost totally vegetarians whose total caloric intake is around twelve hundred a day—hardly American standards.

In Hunza, an agricultural community also, the primary sources of food are vegetables, grains, fruits, and nuts. Most of the time there isn't quite enough to last through a long, hard winter. Many face semi-starvation before the spring thaw comes.

In the Caucasus Dr. Leaf found that the oldsters' diet varies in that here the aged consume animal products daily. There are even some "fatties" over the century mark. These elderly consume about eighteen hundred calories, still less than do most Americans. However, they are meat eaters, much like we are in this country today.

What do the centenarians of these remote villages all have in common then? For one thing they all eat moderate caloric diets, avoid obesity as a rule, and partake of food low in animal and saturated fats. But that's not all. The kicker is: *"The level of physical activity among the aged was very striking in all three areas,"* said Dr. Leaf.

What does that mean in relation to Preventive Care? Dr. Leaf expresses it for us when he says, "I believe that the expenditure of physical energy probably is a better explanation of exceptional longevity than any other influence."

Now anyone for Preventive Care?

Let's take Dr. Leaf's findings one step further. He observed that among these centenarians there is another common denominator. "The old are cherished," Dr. Leaf said. "The older a person is, the higher he or she is regarded both by contemporaries and by the young."

Ah ha. Their elderly are esteemed citizens. They work hard all of their lives and maintain an important part always in the community's social and economic life. "A sense of usefulness and purpose in life pervades the atmosphere," said Dr. Leaf.

And that's what Lawrence Frankel says, too. Those who engage in Preventive Care programs find not only that they are more able, but more willing to return to the mainstream of life again, participate in their community, and then earn "the esteem" of their community forevermore.

Or, to put it another way, as Dr. deVries did at the Appalachian Conference, "There is joy in discovering you still have the capacity to understand, the verve to experiment, the discipline to urge your body to work for you."

If you need more convincing that exercises throughout life must become your new life-style, let Dr. Kaare Rodahl, who was Director of Research at Lankenau Hospital in Philadelphia, Pennsylvania, and a member of the Institute for Work Physiology in Oslo, Norway, speak. He wrote in *Reader's Digest*, May, 1971, his response to those who say, "Why should I exercise? I get along so well without it."

Dr. Rodahl said these people aren't truly honest with themselves. "They are plagued with a good deal of fatigue and frustration for one thing, and their unconditioned bodies are more susceptible than they need be to the organic consequences of stress, such as peptic ulcer, skin ailments, and heart disease. The fact is physical fitness is linked inseparably to personal effectiveness in every field. Anyone willing to take the few simple steps that lie between him and fitness will shortly begin to feel better, and the improvement will reflect itself in every facet of his existence."

Dr. Carl Roncaglione, prominent Charleston physician, has also spoken up. He, along with Frankel, presented a paper on Preventive Care and its magic for aging Americans at the International Congress of Sports, Medicine, and Physical Fitness held in Munich, Germany, concurrently with the twentieth Olympiad in August, 1972. Roncaglione and Frankel presented to this august body their Preventive Care findings and gave case history after case history of its success. They concluded by saying exercise slows aging.

When Dr. Jokl summed up *his* feelings about Charleston's First Appalachian Conference on Aging and on Preventive Care, he told fellow physicans that until recently man believed his physical fitness was structured into a fixed pattern. "Now he knows this is not true. Man knows his is not an unalterable pattern. The individual can largely determine, for himself, how to 'alter' his own pattern and make fitness work wonders for him."

Others who participated in this Appalachian Conference included: Professor Kenneth Redden of the University of Virginia Law School; Dr. Roby Thompson, associate professor of orthopedics, University of Virginia; Dr. Samuel M. Fox III, professor of medicine, George Washington University Medical Center, University Hospital, Washington, D.C.; and Dr. William B. Rossman, fellow, American Psychiatric Association.

One unannounced guest at this conference who brought down the house with her remarks, was Sally T., one of the seventy-two-year olds who helped put on the exercise demonstrations. Dr. Harris asked her to come to the podium and tell the visitors her thoughts on Preventive Care. Sally said, "Larry Frankel had a dream. Now his dream is our dream. We couldn't have started this kind of program without him because he not only was teaching us how to activate our bodies through planned exercise, but how to care what happens to each other. He cares. Without that feeling, that caring, most of us wouldn't be here today."

Apparently, at the First Appalachian Conference, which attracted internationally famous specialists, Preventive Care gained a foothold. All expressed the desire to see the program spread to their own communities.

So, Preventive Care is praised by senators; applauded by businessmen; urged by doctors. It will bring us a nation of healthy old as well as healthy young. It's an action program anyone can implement now.

Certainly there is work going on today in the laboratories around the world to discover the magic pill that will stop aging. But *if* it happens it's still years away, perhaps as many as ten, twenty, or fifty. It won't help those of us who've just discovered a whole batch of new gray hairs, or those whose pants won't close any more, or those who pant now just climbing six stairs. for those the promise of tomorrow isn't good enough. They need help today.

Preventive Care is the answer.

Chapter 14

Preventive Care's Flying Nuns

IT WASN'T JUST a sentimental journey. The retired octogenarian nun who was assisted from the jetliner in her wheelchair wasn't returning to Stevens Point, Wisconsin, that bleak November morning, only because many of her friends over the years would be there. She had come from Cleveland, Ohio, for a definite purpose—to learn to exercise from the confinement of her wheelchair.

More than 225 nuns representing 1200 sisters from the Order of St. Joseph in the states of Ohio, Indiana, Wisconsin, Illinois, and Minnesota, gathered at Stevens Point for their first "Fitness Is Ageless" Conference. The reason? Lawrence Frankel and his team were going to show them how to stay "forever young at heart."

"We were so convinced of the value of the Preventive Care program after attending that First Appalachian Conference in Charleston that we planned our own conference so that our sisters could implement this program in all their provinces," said Sister Madeleine Adamcyzk, S.S.J., General Coordinator of Retirement at St. Joseph Motherhouse in South Bend, Indiana. "The response was way beyond our expectations."

So impressed were the sisters who attended Stevens Point that most went back home to immediately start programs of their own, teaching others in their centers to be instructors for the classes.

"The exercises are so easy to follow that we were easily able

103

Preventive Care participants in Charleston, West Virginia, love to "go calling" on civic and service clubs in downtown areas. Here a group shows its agility during a businessmen's luncheon.

here in South Bend to do a Preventive Care program." Sister Madeleine told me. "We do journey by plane, too, to give workshops, visit other retirement centers, and encourage other groups to start programs like ours."

Sister Madeleine, who speaks with a precise clip to each word that indicated long hours of practice for lecture work, holds a Ph.D. in consulting psychology and is a member of several gerontology groups. She taught in secondary schools and colleges for many years. Seven years ago she decided to specialize in the study of gerontology. She was instrumental in bringing Frankel to her Wisconsin gathering.

Frankel, as the main speaker at Stevens Point, responded to the nuns' enthusiasm for his program by telling them it was a highlight of his career ("My most exciting lecture ever") because they wanted action to spread Preventive Care now. He told them: "In our nation more so than in most nations, giving in to old age had become a socially accepted behavior pattern, as evidenced by the proliferating growth of nursing homes, spiraling numbers in hospitals and extended care facilities, and vast multitudes supported by Government welfare. Your determination to be instrumental in changing this attitude will bring Preventive Care into national focus."

Frankel had Betty Richard, his research associate in exercise planning and design, demonstrate for the sisters exercises that would benefit those in their retirement centers. Betty demonstrated regimens for the neck, shoulders, and hands, as well as strenuous leg exercises and sit-ups. "But don't overdo," Betty told the group. "Stop when you get tired, never overexert yourselves. But try to get into the habit of walking instead of taking an elevator; plan your exercise for specific times, say three times a week, and do them at the same time each day."

All of the representatives at Stevens Point indicated that they would immediately be starting exercise programs in their nursing homes, Motherhouses, and in hospitals they staff.

Frankel stressed to the nuns that they must resist the trend in retirement homes to decline all activity other than watching TV and playing bingo or card games. "Inactivity quite often leads to immobility, the precursor to institutionalization, often in substandard facilities which strike terror in the hearts of so many of our aging."

One sister took Frankel's message seriously enough to implement it that very day. A 'break' was called in the conference, and many dispersed to talk over what they had heard. This sister headed for the elevator to descend to the first floor. Just as she pushed the button she cried out, covered her mouth. Others rushed over to her, thinking she had received an electrical shock. She giggled and said, "I just thought—here I am listening to how to prevent myself and others from aging by using our bodies and I'm going right back to old habits by taking an elevator. I'll *have* to take the stairs."

For the next demonstration at Stevens Point, Frankel, who was constantly stopped by spontaneous applause, called for assistance from the audience to demonstrate exercises. Much like a magician in a theater performance, he called for this audience participation to prove to skeptics that his special brand of "exercise legerdemain" wasn't "tricks" but realistic routines anyone could handle. He pointed to one nun, sitting several rows back.

"No," cried her companion next to her, "she can't. She walks with a cane. She's handicapped."

"Nonsense," said the sister, rising up from her seat, "I can go up there *with* my cane. Why, if I can't do it how am I to teach others?"

Slowly the nun walked down the main aisle to where the speakers were. She walked heavily, leaning on her cane. All eyes were on her. As she reached Betty Richard, she said, "Show me." Betty demonstrated exercises for the head, then did shoulder and arm sets. The nun followed them exactly. The pace increased. The nun was able to do each new exercise. Fifteen minutes passed. When she finished she turned to her audience, smiled, and said, "See, I can do it, so can you." They gave her a standing ovation.

"The directors of our retirement programs are now into full-time programs of Preventive Care in their home states," Sister Madeleine told me. "Not only are they encouraged to give physical fitness regimens to our retired sisters, but many are spreading Preventive Care into every facility they come into contact with. You're right. I guess we are Preventive Care's Flying Nuns because we're willing to go anywhere, anytime, to conduct workshops to show audiences how to stay active all of their lives."

At Sister Madeleine's own Motherhouse in South Bend they use simple equipment—broom handles, rubber balls, mats, a record player, and in some locations, exercise bicycles.

"There are no miracles yet, but we do notice a remarkable change of attitude. Those who once said, 'Oh, I'm too old to do such things,' now say, 'I must keep exercising every day just to keep moving,'" said Sister Madeleine.

Sisters at the Indiana Motherhouse can be seen practicing exercises anywhere, anytime. One eighty-year-old has them all beat. Everyday at breakfast call she's first out in the hall. She waves the rest of them on while she stops to do backbends, holding on to the hall bannister.

Sister Madeleine, who jets from one workshop to another to encourage the aging to make use of their own potential, physically and mentally, has another love now as Director of St. Adalbert Center at Harvest House. It's a new living plan for the elderly that encompasses the idea of usefulness toward others for all the years of one's life.

"It's a whole new approach to involve retired citizens here in Indiana into helping themselves to fulfillment in their sunset years. We want them to get involved with their own peer groups. Preventive Care will be one way of assisting them, because if they feel good, they're ready to step out and do other things. We don't want an elderly 'ghetto,' however. Our Harvest House program will involve all ages of people, young and old alike, in a community spirit of helping each other.

"It actually will be in three stages," the sister explained. "First we'll open neighborhood centers in areas of heavy concentration of older adults, preferably close to a church, where we can rely on permanent headquarters. From this point we can find where older folks live, what their talents and experiences are, and help educate them to the reality *that they are needed*. We will provide for a mutual exchange of services and companionship."

The Harvest House plans, the brainchild of Father Louis J. Putz,

C.S.C., Executive Director, are privately funded, hoping to get people to help themselves to a better life without waiting for Government support.

Sister Madeleine explained, "In Phase II we will provide a new concept of mobile care as an exciting alternative to 'nursing homes.' By getting people together we can organize the elderly into their own association. Then they can care for each other by pooling their own resources. This way those who can, and want to, will remain in their own homes indefinitely. For those with no homes, we hope eventually to provide cooperative living centers at nominal costs. But even in these each resident will be his own master; there will be no monotony of nursing-home care here.

"In Phase III we plan to open a hospital facility to provide maximum care in a pleasant community atmosphere."

An ambitious project? Yes, it is, the sister agreed. "But what is the use of a lifetime of learning, serving, giving, being, if, in old age, you can't utilize it? We want our retired college professors, doctors, and professional people to continue to teach their peers in enrichment courses; house painters long since retired to supervise decorating projects for us while the young come in to do the labor; seamstresses to work on projects desperately needed by others; and people of good cheer to visit those who must be institutionalized to spread their own kind of joy and empathy. We say to the elderly, care about yourself first. Then externalize that feeling to care for others. It will make life worth living into old age."

But the first step, the sister admitted, is to make sure physical-exercise regimens are offered to make people feel good. Then when they do that they'll naturally want to consider projects to mentally stimulate them, too.

From the Retirement Resource Center in Chicago, Illinois, at the Sisters of St. Joseph of the Third Order of St. Francis, Sister Bernice Marie Kogut told me, "Preventive Care exercises began here almost a year ago with the aged and infirm sisters in our provincial home in Bartlett, Illinois. Anywhere from five to nineteen sisters participated in simple low-mobility movements. We use an exercise ball and bamboo sticks to vary our activity. Each week I plan the simple movements with music playing in the background. The music provides a tempo suitable for exercise and encourages them to keep moving.

"We progress slowly because some are not used to any exercise at all for so many years. However, we always are delighted when a sister stops the class to demonstrate how agile she has become."

Sister Bernice told me of one nun who brought with her to class a clipping from a Polish newspaper that described the benefits of simple, daily gymnastics. Gleefully the retired nun reported, "Sister, this article supports all those findings you have been doing with us in Preventicare."

In the fall of '74 and in the years to come, the sisters of St. Joseph plan to lead new workshops to spread the word of Preventive Care. Their message will be to inspire "self-esteem" among their listeners, much like today's popular concept of being your own best friend, and then to have them project this "caring" to all those they encounter.

"Those who like themselves like others," Sister Madeleine said. "If a person has self-esteem he is then able to carry this good feeling into meaningful projects to others. We *can* get a strong force going in the older population. Too often older people think of themselves as 'used up.' Society has encouraged this belief. Now it's time to turn that around. Once we get thousands feeling good again we'll enrich this whole nation."

Another sister who brought back Preventive Care from the Stevens Point conference to her home was Sister Agnes Marie of the St. Joseph Home and Hospital, River Falls, Wisconsin. While she works mostly with those who require skilled care, she feels they, too, thrive when a planned, supervised activity is introduced into their lives.

"We have only broom handles for equipment as most of our residents are in wheelchairs or must remain seated. Music enhances our activity so I plan regimens around slow tunes with a definite beat. I initiated Preventive Care in November, 1973, and have given many lessons since that time. I adapt the program to suit the needs of our people. We meet in the lounge three times a week for one half-hour. All have shown better muscle tone, improved circulation, elimination, and digestion.

"One old gentleman says he comes because he really gets a 'kick' out of it. I ask him, and others who are ambulatory, to join in a circle routine. The standing position does offer more mobility for the body for those who can do it. One of our residents, Phillip, who still drives, said he found the neck-rotation exercises now makes driving comfortable again."

Sister Agnes Marie concluded that Preventive Care added "zest to their years." She has been a physical-education instructor for youth for many years and now she finds giving exercise to the elderly an entirely new challenge.

Along with Sister Madeleine, Sister Mary Juliana, S.S.J., of Stevens Point, has been instrumental in bringing Preventive Care to the retired nuns, setting up conferences, conducting workshops. Sister Juliana implemented Preventive Care at her Motherhouse immediately after visiting Charleston with Sister Madeleine in March of 1973.

"We have organized a class to continue physical exercise and named it 'Fitnic' for fun fitness for all the sisters here at Provincial Home. We meet twice a week. One of our young sisters, a physical-education director, leads us in exercise regimens. We have mats, broomsticks, and other equipment for each participant's use. Now that we are growing, the YMCA had offered its facilities for future classes."

Does Preventive Care work for retired nuns, many of whom never exercised before? So much so that Sister Juliana reported: "Some of our sisters have purchased equipment of their own, like the footpedal pusher, stationary bikes, floor wheels, and other aids, to use daily in their own rooms. The exercise program is at a high pitch here. Even when the weather is bad they go outdoors to walk. They have found what's good about feeling good."

One ninety-year-old retired nun who suffers from chronic heart disease, still exercises. She told me, "Whenever I feel any aches or pains I fight them with my special exercises like I fight the devil himself. I have a strong will to live and I want to enjoy every minute of it."

Another ninety-four-year-old retired sister added, "I sometimes can't get to sleep right away. When that happens I get out of bed, walk the corridor, do some of my exercises to tire me. Before long I'm back in bed and fast asleep." This sister walks and exercises with the aid of a crutch.

"While our Preventive Care program is designed for our own sisters here, we do know it helps others," Sister Juliana reported, "because we expect all of them to keep busy in meaningful projects including crafts and handiwork. We don't believe in retirement per se. Because of this positive approach senility isn't prevalent here. We urge them to keep moving and keep busy."

Sister Felicia Mann, Retirement Director at Marymount Convent in Garfield Heights, Ohio, implemented exercise programs even before she came into contact with Preventive Care's regimens that then reinforced her beliefs. Her classes at the St. Joseph Motherhouse are all done under the direction of a doctor and nurse.

"We find those few who do not take part in our regular exercise program are not as well as they could be . . . those who do take part are able to participate and do enjoy a better feeling toward life."

What's the biggest problem in bringing Preventive Care exercises to those who have never done much physical activity before?

"Getting over the hump of 'I'm too old,'" Sister Felicia said.

"So I ask the sister if she has retired. She'll always answer, 'You know I'm not; that's for old people.' You see, to admit you're retired here is an admission of quitting. So I say to her, 'Okay, you're not too old to try exercise then.' She'll know she was tricked, but at least she'll try the exercises. After that she's hooked."

One sister, age ninety-one, showed them the way. She started down to get on the mat to exercise, but lost her balance. Before anyone could aid her she toppled to the floor. Seeing she wasn't hurt, actually smiling, Sister Felicia told her, "Don't be teaching us an exercise like that. It's only designed to break the floor." The nun got up and went on into the program despite being paralyzed years before in her right arm and leg.

The best part about exercising as one grows older, Sister Felicia went on, is that "it stimulates a positive attitude on the part of our people toward life. Many older people say if they exercise they might harm themselves. It is just the opposite. Those who don't take part find that *not* doing them does more harm.

"It is my hope that soon our Marymount Institute will enlarge its program to provide exercises that will not only help our people develop and maintain their own bodies at a healthful level, but instill in them a positive attitude toward aging."

Even as all of the nuns reported in about the success of their programs of Preventive Care in their home cities, there were plans under way to involve still more. The Flying Nuns who put on exercise workshops are determined to spread the word that Preventive Care can replace Medicare—and it's a lot more fun.

And so the exercise revolution for the aging gains velocity, and more recruits daily. Even now, in large university centers, plans are under way to enlarge already funded Preventive Care's regimens to reach even greater numbers of people. The plan of one such university is detailed in Chapter 16.

Chapter 15

The University of Iowa

TOES HAS NOTHING whatsoever to do with reaching down and touching all ten of them. Rather it's an acronym meaning "The Oaknoll Exercise Society," the name of the group of seniors at an Iowa City retirement home who sparked that state's involvement in a Preventive Care-like program of exercise.

The co-leaders of TOES are Drs. David K. Leslie and John W. McLure, assistant professors in the Department of Physical Education at the University of Iowa.

Their program all started on a hot, summer day in 1971 during a graduate class in curriculum on the university campus. The professor was Dr. McLure. The subject for the day—inter-generational togetherness—or apartness, depending on your point of view.

One graduate student thought out loud: "I wonder what our older citizens really *could* contribute to our society if we, all of us, the rest of society, suddenly tapped their talents?"

Dr. McLure answered, "Let's ask them." He arranged for the students to meet Iowans in retirement at Oaknoll in a rap session. The home's oldsters were plain-spoken and quite articulate in their needs. One spelled it out for them: "We want most of all an exercise program. Not just busy little things to do but a real calisthenic program that will make us feel so good we'll want to continue it for the rest of our lives."

They were so enthusiastic in their demand for such a program that Dr. McLure became excited about it, too. He took their plan to his colleague, Dave Leslie. Both agreed it was not only workable but highly desirable and much needed.

Preventive Care's Flying Nuns are just as good on the dance floor as they are on the lecture circuit. Here, in an evening session in Stevens Point, Wisconsin, after a day of demonstration in their "Fitness Is Ageless" clinic, all participate in a lively folk dance.

By November of 1971 TOES was under way. At first it was held just on Tuesdays with the "T" in TOES standing for *that* day. More than sixty residents at Oaknoll signed up for the class and in their enthusiasm pressed the professors for more time.

"One day a week isn't enough to maintain fitness," the residents said. Both leaders agreed.

Fridays were chosen as the second day of the week to stage the exercise pilot program that both men hoped would spread to other retirement centers and nursing homes. Eventually thirteen residents and homes were included in the TOES program as funding and additional help became available.

"In some homes the participants were ambulatory and in others they were not. Exercise sessions later lasted between thirty and forty minutes, depending upon many variables," Dr. Leslie explained. "Unlike Preventive Care, we avoided activities that stressed the cardio-vascular system because of limitations in our screening system. This is a major limitation to the program, and one which I would like to see remedied later on.

"What we do in our exercise sessions is stress routines that benefit the senior resident by improving or maintaining muscle tone, flexibility, balance, posture, and a feeling of well-being while providing socializing activities. An effort is made to stimulate a full range of movement at all joints. Typically the class averages about fifteen participants."

Shortly after TOES was implemented at Oaknoll, the Iowa Foundation granted the pilot project two hundred dollars for needed supplies, including hand exercisers to improve grip, strength, and flexibility; a shoulder wheel to encourage full range of arm movement; and chest and arm exercises for muscle tone and strength.

"One very strong man in our class really took us by surprise," Dr. Leslie remembered. "We tested him with a hand-grip machine and he scored well. After a few months in the program he did even better.

While we knew he was benefiting from the fitness class, he volunteered another answer: "I've been a minister all of my life, you see. And everyone knows a minister spends his life shaking hands so naturally he must have a good grip on people, too."

At first the classes at Oaknoll pre-empted almost every other activity. For some, even their ice cream melted.

As it worked out, Drs. Leslie and McLure scheduled their Tuesday exercise class for the hour when the bus brought residents back from the grocery store, carts and all. Seeing their favorite class about to begin, many hurried into the exercise room, "parking" their carts nearby. It wasn't unusual to see one or two oldsters peel out of an exercise formation, grab brownbags containing ice cream, and rush the perishable item to the refrigerator freezers in their apartments.

"It wasn't long and the word got out that we were giving these people a new outlook on life," Dr. Leslie said. "Other nursing homes and retirement centers wanted us immediately to start similar programs at their centers. At that time we couldn't."

But then the news that grant money might be available to assist the educators in expanding their program came. "Our TOES program was initiated in 1971. Two years later, in 1973, the Commission on Aging in Iowa, through Title III of the Older Americans Act, funded us eighteen thousand dollars for a one-year pilot program, which ends in August of 1974. We're now exploring the possibility of a renewal or an application for a much larger and more extensive health-care package for greater numbers," said Dr. Leslie.

"We aren't going to just let it drop. There is a vital interest in the program. We've been in touch with Mr. Frankel and his foundation and hope to coordinate all of his material with our own to enlarge our program here.

"Both John and I now know our older citizens benefit from a program of regular, organized group exercises. It helps them maintain a vigorous level of physical fitness," both commented in an article they wrote for *Johpher* magazine.

The initial classes started at Oaknoll, which later became a demonstration group with an age range from sixty-six to ninety-three. University graduate students majoring in physical education assisted with the expanded programs; they offered to serve both as leaders of exercise routines and as data keepers, and made notes that would help them in their own studies of needs of all ages in the population for physical activity on a planned, supervised basis.

"Right now we are preparing an illustrated booklet for the Commission of Aging on the results of our programs growing out of the TOES project. We served a seven-county area and hope to expand to cover all of Eastern Iowa."

The retirement and nursing homes that participate in the University of Iowa project of exercise for the elderly are within a sixty-mile radius (one way) of the campus. "One of the main program objectives of expanding TOES for our state is to train seniors as their own physical-activity leaders to serve in their retirement and nursing homes. With a sum appropriated for their salaries, there will be an incentive for them to provide for their peer group. But it will not just be a job, it will be a calling."

In addition to the exercise equipment purchased with the foundation money, TOES also had a variety of rubber bouncing balls for use in relays, games, and individual workouts. The group, whenever possible, did their routines to music provided by casettes, as in Preventive Care classes.

What are some of the short- and long-range goals of TOES?

Dr. Leslie responded: "We initially wanted to develop a physical-activity program for older citizens designed to maintain or restore physical fitness to levels that assist these seniors in carrying out their activities of daily living with reasonable efficiency and enthusiasm.

"We also wanted to produce this illustrated booklet to describe our activities, give group leadership training guidelines, and offer organizational and administrative suggestions for anyone wanting to implement a program similar to ours."

Dr. Leslie keeps in close touch with Frankel and his foundation, having visited Charleston and seen the revolution Preventive Care seeded. Dr. Leslie wants this kind of West Virginia enthusiasm to sweep his home state, too, so that all its older citizens can participate in a new, independent life-style.

Long-range goals of TOES include:

1. The establishment of an exercise program-demonstration model group that is centrally located, mobile, and ready to move into any other retirement center that requests demonstrations.

2. The creation of opportunities among these elderly for increased contact of a socializing nature among themselves and with college-age students.

3. The development of a pool of leadership talent capable of expanding more physical-activity programs for more senior groups. TOES wants the leadership to come both from the seniors' peer groups and from college physical-education majors, to narrow the generation gap.

That's only for openers. Drs. Leslie and McLure envision a rainbow on the horizon that offers:

1. A self-perpetuating physical-activity program in retirement and nursing homes for all seniors in Iowa.

2. Exercises to accommodate the needs of all seniors regardless of state of mobility. That means if they can walk they can exercise; if they can't they still can exercise—and feel better for it.

3. An opportunity for physicians to view TOES classes or come to orientation lectures to hear what fine results they are getting. The doctors would be asked to guide the program to make it even more beneficial to all.

4. The immediate availability of a program for every retirement center that wants it.

5. Work that will fuse the cultures of the very young—junior high and up—with the very old, to establish empathy among both generations for each other.

Since TOES expanded from the one-day-a-week classes in 1971 to today's refined programs under Title III, more than five hundred seniors have been involved in classes.

And their numbers are multiplying. Like Preventive Care, once you get an older person fit and able, there's no limit to his own personal goals. He then wants very much to live, to work, to play, and because he feels so good, to help others join the Revolution.

"Earlier in our program of trying to bring TOES into the mainstream of life we decided to involve high-school students from our area in our program," Dr. Leslie said. "We have in our city a West High School that has a group of teens called CORE. They are not only from West High, but from all other secondary schools in Iowa City.

"The CORE teens have one thing in common—they hate physical-education classes as they are taught in their own schools. The formal, do-this-do-that kind of program really turns them off.

Everyone was searching for another kind of program that would show these kids that physical education *is* important—it's also a life-style.

"What better way, we thought, than to bring these CORE youngsters to Oaknoll so they could see how important exercise is to seniors? So we did. The students were brought over to Oaknoll to act as leaders in exercise routines or as helpers in any way needed. We wanted them to relate to the older people and understand something of others' needs, too."

Did it work?

"While it's hard to evaluate the project in terms of statistics, yes, I think it did. Why? Because some of the youngsters, after the program was over, went back, on their own, to Oaknoll to help out in a clinical way. Sure, others viewed it as a chance to 'get away from school' or 'sneak a smoke,' but not the majority. It revealed there was some real rapport between the two groups."

So much so that Drs. Leslie and McLure are now planning to enlarge this kind of youth-age program of physical fitness into a much more sophisticated program later on in 1974 and 1975, this time involving youngsters from junior as well as senior high school.

With TOES now three years old and growing, not only into more exercise programs for the elderly, but in fostering intergenerational groups aimed at bringing back empathy of the young for the old and vice versa, what have the University of Iowa's professors learned thus far?

"Exercise is needed and wanted by all older Americans, even if many don't say so. After they get into a program with their peers, they find they have a brighter outlook on life, really enjoy themselves, feel much better. And the chasm between generations shrinks."

During their visits to the retirement and nursing homes, Drs. Leslie and McLure heard all kinds of comments. Most of them revolved around weight loss in pounds as well as inches. At almost any session they heard, "Look, my dress is now too big for me," or "Three weeks ago I could only do that exercise three times. This week I can go seven. And my trousers are loose on me."

One thing the professors and their graduate students did notice. The attitudes are quite different at retirement centers from those at nursing homes. They could see, like Lawrence Frankel, that at nursing homes they were there "later than they should have been, but earlier than they could have been."

Dr. Leslie added, "At some nursing homes they've almost given up. They're already quite ill. It's difficult to develop leadership from their peer group because of prolonged poor health and there isn't funding for staff personnel to carry out long-term exercise programs of their own.

"Now at retirement centers, they are really enthusiastic and want to learn more each time we meet."

One point common to all the people both in TOES and Preventive Care classes was that they all have found reserves of strength, stamina, and endurance they didn't even know they had before.

"All seniors in our University of Iowa TOES program enjoyed meeting with others their own age and with those generations younger. This feeling is genuine." Dr. Leslie said, "A friendly pat on the shoulder, a handshake, a steadying hand during a routine—all of this means *touching*. That's important. The young in our program soon find out what their older friends learned long ago—love is still the most important visitor in the classroom."

Two graduate students were vital to the University of Iowa's TOES project—George Frekany, a doctoral candidate in physical education, and Amelia Winterfeld, working for her Master of Arts degree in therapeutic recreation.

What advice would Drs. Leslie and McLure have for other universities or even private citizens who want to start a regimen of low-mobility exercise either in a class or for themselves?

Like Preventive Care, the TOES leaders insist that any person who wants to start now on a life-style of exercise must first get his or her physician's consent. Let him determine restrictions, if any, that one should follow. Then, like Frankel, the professors agree that music during exercise adds to the enjoyment of any class or private session.

"When we go into a retirement home we found it is far better to run off announcements of the exercise classes and have them distributed in advance to each resident, personally," Dr. Leslie said. He explained this was much preferred to posting isolated notices, like on a lobby bulletin board, because the individual notices are sure to reach the handicapped and semi-invalids.

A demonstration program, such as Frankel uses in his Charleston program, and the professors use in TOES' Iowa project, is another must. Both have developed a mobile group that is "on call" to show peers that exercise isn't a drudgery, but a joy.

While Preventive Care has a full-time medical committee as part of its board of directors to work closely with all classes in that program, TOES leaders also stay in close contact with their medical community.

Classes for exercises should be held in a location that is easy to reach for seniors. In one of the Preventive Care programs the Sisters of St. Joseph initiated in their state, they arranged for buses to pick up those who couldn't walk to their classes, or arranged for car pools among the peer groups to help each other get there.

All classes—Preventive Care, TOES, and the others that spring up around the nation—must remain flexible, Dr. Leslie pointed out. Participants, he felt, should be free to drop in and out as personal needs dictate.

All agree a regular meeting time should be chosen and carefully maintained. This is important whether it is for a class or for an individual doing exercise routines of his own.

The length of time for classes can vary. Most of the TOES groups meet for thirty to forty minutes. Dr. Leslie explained: "This limit is especially important due to the presence of a variety of restrictive physical conditions of the group. Even with a graduated set of exercises, there are bound to be some people present at almost any meeting who are still at the beginning level or who have been ill and must work back to their former level of participation."

All leaders agree that repetition is a must in calling out routines. The speed of a class should be adjusted to its beginners, not the advanced. Like the cream in milk, achievers always will rise to the top naturally, regardless of the tempo.

When a class is performing, or if someone is working on exercises like those in Chapter 20 of this book, limits should be observed. In a class situation it is up to the leader to call out the number of repetitions for any one exercise. At a beginner level, he must say, "That's enough for those of you just starting. The others can do five more." If you are alone, you must start at the lowest number recommended, and work up.

At the TOES programs, they find team teaching advantageous.

While one leads the majority of the class in exercise routines, the other instructor helps those people who have special needs, like those in wheelchairs or walkers. The second leader also can assist in gathering data, offer encouragement, and compare important notes with the other instructor after the session is over.

Variety and routine were and are paramount in the TOES programs. While favorite routines are always in demand, TOES leaders encourage instructors to try various new games or exercises that might stimulate the group.

And Dr. Leslie and Frankel are adamant in encouraging socializing before, during, and after classes. Preventive Care or TOES should be a socially pleasant encounter, a way to bring together both old and new friends.

TOES encourages those participating in the exercise classes to volunteer as leaders. Then, too, Dr. Leslie added, "Do applaud, recognize, and encourage the person who suggests a reaching movement to use in making up beds or another who thinks of exercising the hands by wringing out a wet towel."

One final but important aspect carried out in both TOES and Preventive Care programs is the distribution of proficiency awards. In TOES (see Appendix) certificates are given out to those who complete a given number of classes or attain real proficiency. In Preventive Care trophies are often awarded for achievement. Both programs agree that awards are morale boosters that shouldn't be forgotten or overlooked in building a program.

Lawrence Frankel initiated his Preventive Care program in 1970. He invited educators like Drs. Leslie and McLure to visit, to explore, and to share knowledge. Because he did, the concept of Preventive Care is spreading. It's for the old, for the young, for the well, for the lame. Great universities are now embracing it. It says to all of us, stay well, stay fit. And, then, help others to feel as good as you do.

Didn't someone else once say that, too, a long time ago? Didn't it go, "Do unto others. . . ."?

Chapter 16

"Try It, You'll Like It"

FOR SENIORS LIVING in Montana, Preventive Care-type programs had to be "show and tell." Only then, they told educators, if they liked what they saw, would they be willing to go into a fitness program and spread to others that exercise should be a way of life.

Aware of their attitude of "show me" and their age-old habit of viewing with suspicion any program funded by the Government, the University of Montana, excited by the concept of Preventive Care, decided to work out its own program of physical fitness for the elderly, *then* get local citizens behind it. The leader of the program in the university's recreation department was Dr. Lloyd Heywood. His assistants were graduate students from his department, led by Miss Barbara Day, candidate for a master's degree.

In Montana the targets were the sixty-six senior centers throughout the state. All were informed that the university had under way a program for the elderly that would help bring them back to life with vigor and renewed interest in themselves and their community.

But there *was* a catch. The university told the directors at the senior centers such a program was possible but that each center would have to meet certain criteria in order to participate. In effect the university was playing the reluctant bride.

The rules weren't hard, just practical to help break through that stigma of "Government programming." First, the director of the local senior center had to personally make a request for a demonstration of the exercise program with the university. And the di-

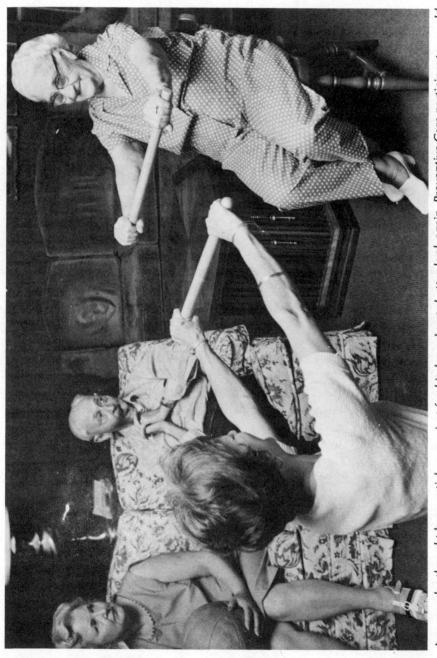

Anyone who thought broomsticks were just for kitchen closets better look again. Preventive Care participants use old broom handles, cut to fourteen inches, to do exercise routines. Here at a retirement home, Betty Richard of the Frankel Foundation shows a group how to do broomhandle exercises.

rector had to assure them they had set up a full day's workshop, inviting the local school superintendent, several physical-education teachers, and seniors who might become leaders for this program for their peers.

Once a center set the works into motion, Barbara Day or one of her assistants would visit them, "show and tell" the program of exercises for the elderly, and suggest ways to implement it.

"The only way to reach people is to go directly to them," Dr. Heywood said. "You can have the best program in the world but if you don't talk to them face-to-face, share their problems, and listen to their doubts, your program is doomed to failure. There is no substitute for that one-to-one approach—it's caring as well as sharing."

Barbara found the legend of proud Montanans to be true. Yet, no matter where she went, the enthusiasm for the exercise program snowballed.

Under the Title III, Older Americans Act, the University of Montana received from the Government $55,131 to do a year's pilot program offering physical activities for the aging. Of this amount, $13,783 was the university's personal share. The grant ran from April, 1973, to April, 1974, and was then extended to continue through August of 1974.

"And we won't let it stop there," Dr. Heywood said. "We feel now that we've brought this program to thirty some odd centers who requested it, we have an important start in reaching the elderly. We plan to seek additional funds to try to reach all of the sixty-six senior centers, hoping in turn they will spread the word to others so that other programs similar to ours can reach everyone who wants it."

Barbara visited all over Montana to hear what the elderly had to say about exercise, about recreation, about living. She offered her expertise in exchange for their knowledge how best to teach others, bring them all into the program. She often told them that the university's program was really not anything radically new, just an extension of what everyone, even seniors, knew all along, just finally brought together into a packaged program all now could share.

The seniors got the message. Of the more than thirty centers requesting the university program, all now have working programs in physical fitness and hope to expand in the months and years to come.

One piece of equipment was often requested, a stationary bicycle. The university, through its strong buying power, provided it. Working with a sympathetic manufacturer, they were able to get bicycles for the centers that requested them at a fantastically low price—by buying in large volume. They said others could do the same by buying needed equipment in quantity, through one central clearing house. In this case it was the university.

The immediate one-year goal of the University of Montana's program of physical fitness for the elderly was to provide a regimen of exercises that were primarily therapeutic in nature.

Did they?

"While we have no statistical data as yet to confirm it, we know it has worked. When people seek you out, talk to you about how their lives have been changed, how good they feel, and tell you about all of their plans for the future, you know you've changed their life-style," Dr. Heywood said. "Our assistants working in the field were right there to see and hear how our program worked. They felt, wherever they went, a sense of renewed vigor in the lives of the maturing Montanan."

Part of the university's grant money went for salaries to the graduate assistants and to pay for their travel to and from the senior centers. Small salaries were paid to seniors who offered to act as leaders in their own centers to keep the physical-fitness program in force. In that respect the University of Montana program was doing in its state what Preventive Care hopes to do for the nation. Preventive Care, by training its "missionaries" from the peer group of the elderly to go out and teach others in the community, hopes every American who wants to do an about-face and be fit in his old age will have the chance to get into a program *now*.

Like Preventive Care, the University of Montana sought a "special" kind of peer group leader, too. Said Dr. Heywood, "We know now that the person leading this program of physical fitness for the elderly must be a rather outstanding and unique kind of personality. Leadership qualities alone aren't enough. The person who works in our program must radiate good will and empathy for the older citizen. The leader must be one who can move an older person who has never exercised before in his entire life to now *want* to exercise more than anything else. That's not an easy thing. But seeing is doing. If the leader is past fifty-five, in excellent health, fit and trim, his "student" will be saying, 'If he can do it, I can too.' "

What Dr. Heywood was saying was that the leaders in any program for the elderly must never patronize them, but empathize with them instead. He must show real love, concern, and caring.

"Now that our program is in full force, we'll depend heavily on our local leaders to keep their programs alive. If they've done a good job at the start, the participants themselves will never let it drop. After all, when you feel good now and last year you felt just awful, you're going to fight to keep what you've got. We're counting on that."

Other large institutions, as well as universities and retirement homes, have implemented Preventive Care on programs similar to it in nature. One of these large facilities that is deep into Preventive Care practices today is Weston State Hospital in Weston, West Virginia. Located close to Charleston, they heard about what Frankel was doing recycling the old bodies for new, and they felt sure most of their thirteen hundred hospitalized people could benefit from a regimen of exercise.

One of the staff, C. Gene Furbee, clinical psychologist of the Medicare Unit, referred to Preventive Care as a "neat balance of science, practicality, and humanism." His conclusions were echoed by Dr. Richard Bracco, the clinical director of the hospital. Not only did they decide to bring exercise to the hospital patients, but both men indicated all of their staff, too, would participate in a stepped-up program of physical exercise for themselves.

Of the thirteen hundred patients, more than a fourth of them at Weston are age sixty-five and over. The influence of Preventive Care's exercises on them has been excellent and the program is now in a stage of expansion.

The University of Louisville also has tasted success with exercise for the elderly. While its program was not Government funded, and lacked the long-range planning it needed to last, it did open the doors for the seniors themselves to take hold and seek help to get future funding to make exercise a part of that city's retired people's everyday lives.

Two students, Nina Pound and Joyce Weisrock, working with instructor Grace Backmeier of the school's physical-education department, worked out a program of exercises for the elderly, then took their plan to the head of a retirement residence in their city, Mrs. Kirby Stoll of Senior House. What the young women wanted to do was lead these seniors into a program of low-mobility exercises, then find peer leaders to carry it on.

There was great initial interest. A local television station televised the classes in a news special. Many testimonials from the elderly poured in. One woman, age ninety-three, couldn't wait to tell her views on camera. "I've never been so excited by a program in years. I guess it was always something we wanted and been waiting for and just didn't know it. Not only does exercise make me feel better, it gives me a chance to get out, meet others. I love it."

Unfortunately, the program hasn't expanded in that city because there was no long-term planning for it in anyone's budget. However, the idea sparked interest and the climate now is favorable in Louisville—an open invitation for a Preventive Care "missionary" to step in and tie up the loose strings. What this city (and others like it) needs is a "parent" group, like Preventive Care, to work out the regimens, offer leadership, and the commitment of long-term support, to get the programs to the people who need them the most.

Now, what about nutrition?

As Preventive Care spreads, the question always comes up, "What about the oldsters who are now obese? Will this program bring their weight in line?"

Everyone agrees—doctors, educators, and Preventive Care's Frankel Foundation—that physical fitness and trim bodies go hand in hand. Those who now have an overweight problem are going to have to face it and solve it now. To be physically fit you have to maintain a normal weight, too. One can't happen without the other. They're happily wedded in concept.

All right, you say, then give me help to lose weight.

To begin with, it won't happen overnight.

If it's taken you sixty-five years to add sixty pounds over your ideal weight, exercise alone isn't going to take it off. Of course, it will help trim and tighten those muscles, but since you ate yourself into overweight it's up to you now to lose that weight the same way—undereat.

How?

There's no easy way. Visit your doctor first, and when you obtain his permission to exercise, you can ask him to work with you on a healthful program to shed pounds. He knows your physical condition, your past medical history, your personal hangups. He can best determine a plan.

But plans don't take off pounds. If you are determined to lose weight, you will. If you like the sound of the words but enjoy heaping bowls of vanilla ice cream more, you're not going to make it.

The New life-style encompasses a total outlook—a fit body and a trim one. Working out with a low-mobility exercise plan while you diet will help you achieve a state where you can greet each day with renewed vigor. Make that your goal.

One doctor who heads the nutrition research for a national livestock and meat board, Dr. William C. Sherman, observed that most people who are physically inactive are likely to become obese. He said, "Men, women, and children who are physically active spontaneously adjust their food intake and maintain relatively constant weight; however, there is evidence that inactive people do not adjust their appetite to a lower level and their voluntary food intake is greater than is needed to remain in caloric balance. For the inactive person, *increased physical activity is the only alternative* to a lifetime of semi-starvation and hunger or to obesity.

"There is a great need for increased emphasis in our school systems on the importance of a regular exercise routine to be continued throughout life and at a level sufficient to maintain a reasonable degree of physical fitness."

"Many people believe that the calories used in exercise are insufficient to be of much value, but even two hours a day of walking three miles an hour uses three hundred to four hundred calories more than sitting . . . moderate exercise also is important in maintaining muscle tone."

There are many books, some of which are listed in this book's bibliography, that point the way to self-study of good nutrition, if one wants to explore it in depth. However, if you are looking for a kind of "fun" book, geared to retired couples who want good nutrition *and* a diet to help them lose weight, Charles N. Aronson wrote and published one called *Regimen.*

A retired New York machine-company executive, Mr. Aronson decided after he retired to find out as much as he could about good nutrition and diet. His motive was selfish—he wanted to lose weight.

Aronson investigated all of the popular crash diets, wrote to various companies for their brochures on good nutrition, read all the current material available. His conclusion: If you want to lose weight, you can, and will; if you don't, no crash diet will help because the pounds will be back on almost immediately after you stop dieting on that plan.

So what's a retired person to do who has too much time on his hands and too many temptations to snack or to cook up delicious meals?

Aronson said, "Eat all you want of *good* food, skip all the snacks. But feed yourself only twice a day. I did and went from 218 pounds to my best weight of 180. And what's more, I've stayed there."

Regimen's diet rules are really quite simple. You decide for yourself what times of the day you will eat those two meals. You eat all of the good things you're used to eating with the exception of pastries, candies, and snack foods. They're out. And you cannot eat immediately after a meal or at any time in-between.

The *Regimen* diet of two meals a day doesn't require counting calories. You eat all kinds of meat, poultry, mashed potatoes with gravy, spaghetti, vegetables, and salads—all the good food you're used to.

"Being a scientist (designer and mechanical engineer), I knew that when the *Regimen* had slimmed me down to near my true best weight, the weight loss would lessen and finally stop entirely," Aronson said, "and that's exactly what happened."

This retired New Yorker is opposed to all crash and fad diets for seniors because they just don't work for a long span of time. Many diets fail, too, Aronson stated, because they are bland, taste-less, boring, and offer only foods ordinarily foreign to you or ones you have a real dislike for. The natural way to diet is to eat good foods you really like. And, Aronson said, there's nothing wrong with a martini or two before dinner.

But he's death on "appetizers," the tempters that go along with the before-dinner drink. "Have you ever heard of anything more ridiculous? You have two 180-calorie martinis, dunk 16 potato chips into an onion dip you can't leave alone, and pretty quick you've taken up 700 calories in order to work up an 'appetite' to finish off a 2,000-calorie dinner."

Regimen's author recommends two meals a day for retired couples, scheduled between 9 or 10 A.M. and again between 4 and 5 P.M. Working people who try this diet would have to adjust to their own best times.

Allowable "lifts" during the day include steaming hot cups of beef bouillon, tea, or coffee, or a sugar-free diet drink. A calorie count per ounce for every drinkable liquid is given in one of the many tables of food values included in his book.

Menus, too, are suggested by Aronson, who admits to being somewhat of a gourmet in the kitchen. He likes to grind his own hamburger and make his own pork sausage from scratch. His personal menus won't remind anyone that they are dieting. He observed: "Nobody pushed food down your throat. Nobody else, that is. You got heavy because you ate too much. The only way you'll get 'unheavy' is to eat a little too little. A varied, well-balanced diet doesn't just solve the problem of overweight, it prevents the occurrence of the problem."

The major factor in maintaining normal weight, according to all the experts on nutrition is to eat a well-balanced diet and to avoid an excess in calories. Dr. Jean Mayer, who is the Presidential advisor on nutrition; Dr. George W. Irving, administrator of the U.S. Department of Agriculture's Research Service; and Dr. Charles Glen King, professor emeritus of Columbia University's Institute of Human Nutrition, all reiterate that good nutrition is important to all people who diet, but vital to the elderly who want to shed pounds.

Dr. Robert E. Taylor, in his book, *Feeling Alive After 65*, offers retired people a three-meal-a-day plan designed to effect a safe weight loss of two pounds a week. His suggested menus give protein, vitamins, and other necessary nutrients, yet avoid all high-calorie foods. He insists, as others do, that there be no snacking between meals.

He adds, "Staying slim requires day-to-day diet planning. Youthful follies of chocolate cake, ice cream, and candy are gone forever. While the older person may allow himself a rare treat, a weight problem can be avoided only by strict adherence to a diet of meat, fish, vegetables, fresh fruits, and some dairy products. Only constant vigilance can prevent obesity."

In losing weight, and maintaining your ideal weight, select a lifetime plan to follow. Whether it's two balanced meals a day or three, counting calories, the important first step is a consultation with your doctor. Let him help you to determine what your ideal weight is and suggest how you can get there and stay there.

Then once you are on a diet plan for life, or better yet, a good eating plan for optimum health, and you're exercising regularly along with it, you're well on your way to creating a life-style for yourself that will bring you into a healthful old age. You'll look toward your mature years as a time of continued challenge in which you will play a vital role, not as a spectator, but as a vocal participant—one whose voice can and will be heard.

Chapter 17

The Future of Preventive Care

A GROWING NUMBER of physicians invoved in geriatrics now believe that the only untried approach toward increasing life expectancy is through overt action—exercise—to slow down the aging process. This process, many believe, should result in putting off heart attacks, cancer, and strokes, so as to permit the elderly years more of healthful living.

That's the premise under which Frankel initiated Preventive Care. The entire state of West Virginia has caught fire with this movement of making exercise a way of life not only for its elderly, but for all those people past middle age who never before included physical activity as a main component of their lives.

Today Frankel is much in demand as a speaker everywhere in his adopted state not only to tell of the phenomenal results of exercise in the deceleration of aging, but to set up Preventive Care programs for city groups, rural groups, hospitals, and nursing homes. From this deluge of demand for help and because of the excitement it has generated, the Frankel Foundation's board of directors has pledged its expertise and that of its medical advisory committee to bring Preventive Care's benefits to the nation by providing trained personnel, lectures, and demonstration projects.

"The key to our program is an interchange of love and affection to show that we care," Frankel said. "Without that ingredient it is impossible to motivate older people who are already depressed and withdrawn."

Where to begin?

Right now, new programs in Preventive Care are mushroom-

You are never too old to exercise. This man, at seventy-two, works out three times a week in the Charleston, West Virginia, gym, including doing head stands on the rings.

ing in and around Charleston and up and down that state. Frankel thinks his West Virginia should have the top priority in establishing Preventive Care as a way of life for all of its older citizens, and then serve as a model for the rest of the nation.

Then what?

"The investment of a million will save a billion," he pointed out. The foundation wants the United States Government to invest in the good health of its aging population through preventive medicine—Preventive Care. Frankel will train peer groups of "missionaries," trained physical education instructors, to carry back to their own communities all over the nation the regimen of planned, supervised, low-mobility exercise. Frankel wants Preventive Care to get there first, before Medicare has to take over.

"The Government could save its taxpayers billions of dollars it now uses to subsidize custodial institutions and to send out literature that never reaches the right people, by investing in the health of its older people, bringing them back into our mainstream of living to be productive, first-class, involved citizens contributing to society instead of draining it."

Then what's the plan?

After the foundation gets both Government funds and some private support from philanthropic foundations interested in problems of the aging, it will undertake building a huge, modern facility in Charleston. It will be headquarters for training all "missionary" personnel for Preventive Care under the supervision of the original team composed of Frankel, Betty Richard, and Beulah Phillips.

Right now the Frankel Foundation is interviewing men, one of whom will become Frankel's successor someday. He will be trained not only in the skills and techniques of the program, but in the philosophy of caring, so important in making this program work. Betty and Beulah will assist him and Frankel in training personnel both as instructors and nurses for the rest of America.

"Our Preventive Care 'missionaires' cannot be just ordinary people interested in physical fitness," Frankel said. "They must have the zeal of a missionary to carry the word of physical fitness in much the same way as those did who carried the word of Christianity in early times. We want them eventually to be in the same age group as those they plan to teach. They will need a loving and caring personality. It will take a lot of screening."

Acquiring this expanded facility to train these people has top priority with the Frankel Foundation's board of directors. Guy Erwin, president, said, "We already have an option on a building site for our use. We also have a chance to acquire a structure not now in use which we could remodel to suit our needs. Either way we will be ready to go in just a short while. We must consider a site that is centrally located in Charleston so that all of our older citizens can reach it with ease."

How soon can the public expect the new headquarters to be ready?

"We hope to have it going within two years," Erwin said. "However, if we get Government and foundation backing in 1974, we should be able to accelerate our plans and get our new building in time to start training people in Preventive Care systems early in 1975."

Once the new building is ready, Frankel will invite interested persons from various groups around the country who already have asked for training to come to Charleston and learn how to take Preventive Care back to their own communities.

Preventive Care administrators also will work closely with senior clubs, housing programs for the elderly, recreation centers, city and county governments, and state and county medical societies. A cooperative arrangement with local health departments for the utilization of their services would be valuable.

But that procedure alone won't reach all Americans, and that concerns the board. Newspapers, magazine articles, and books help incite the revolution, but more of an audience is needed to keep it alive.

A vast public-information program will be used to bring Preventicare to America. Newspapers, radio, and television will be utilized toward this end. Because Frankel is in demand as a speaker now almost to his capacity, other lecture bureaus will be established to bring the message of this program to every club that asks. The senior clubs of America will be a major vehicle in the public-relations scheme.

"We hope to produce, perhaps with private foundation money or a commercial sponsor, a television Preventive Care exercise program on a major network daily or at least three times a week for all aging Americans. Our exercises will be for all those over fifty who want to stay fit and also for the handicapped, for those confined to wheelchairs or to their beds, and for those who must not walk too often.

"In a fifteen-minute show we could reach millions and graphically demonstrate, with our 'peer group' instructors, all of the exercises one can do in his own home. We could stress on such a show that everyone participating must first get their physician's approval, just as we do in the classes here in Charleston."

An outreach effort also is planned for minority groups and for the elderly now in low-income areas. This will be accomplished through participation of residents of housing projects for the elderly as well as other housing Federally and state supported.

For example, a showcase program for low-income elderly is now under way in the North Charleston Community Center. It will provide a prototype for other programs. More than 75 percent of the elderly now enrolled in the Preventive Care programs in Kanawha County are in this category. With a minimum investment in equipment, the Preventive Care format can easily be adapted for use also in resident complexes, church recreation centers, and school multi-purpose rooms.

Basically all one really needs to start a program is a place to exercise. For each participant they would need two one-pound dumbbells or two one-pound cans of vegetables, a fourteen-inch piece of broomstick, and a mat or pad to do the routines on in comfort. Almost any budget can provide that.

What a delight it would be, and what a victory for Preventive Care, if from this day forward the blueprints of all Federally supported low-income housing projects for the elderly would have a multi-purpose room for exercise. What an incentive that would be to get this program cracking.

As Preventive Care grows, each community will need its own advisory committee. It should consist of three leading members of the community, a medical-advisory committee, six elderly consumers, representatives of Social Security, vocational rehabilitation, and Title III projects of the Commission on Aging.

This committee could make recommendations regarding methods of achieving Preventive Care objectives, and would serve in a public-relations capacity, and to advise their projects director in their city.

Every six or twelve months, formal evaluation on the Preventive Care program would be made in each community that adopts it. In-between, frequent informal reviews of the on-going program should be made in order to spot real success and failures, to find why these are so, and to ascertain the direction in which the program is moving. Flexibility will be the key word.

"In some instances, figures may form the basis of evaluation," Frankel explained. "In others, the judgment may be more subjectively measured by attitudes, better health, and preventive aspects."

Financial support for the Frankel Foundation now comes not only from the state's Commission on Aging but from private donations. The tax-exempt foundation will continue to accept the public's support to maintain its present programs and also await nationwide funding.

What then? Where will Preventive Care go when it's hooked the nation's aging?

To the young.

Frankel wants the young to relate to the aging population, to make them proud of their parents, their grandparents, and all older citizens.

"I'd like to see our nation's young people whip out their wallets and show pictures of their grandparents to their friends instead of the other way around. Nowadays we can't talk ten minutes to a proud older person without him showing pictures of his or her grandchildren. That's great. But now it's time to reverse the action."

Frankel wants to open up all those old peoples' ghettos where the residents not only don't relate to each other, but never see the young.

"We want to go to high schools and colleges and urge youngsters to adopt a grandparent if they don't already have one, or even if they do. We'd like them to visit retirement homes and communities and pick a grandparent they can visit regularly.

"This wouldn't be the patronizing kinds of visits that seem to abound today. These would be stimulating exchanges of communication. The young people would talk on politics, problems of the community, their problems, coming elections, news in music, theater, and the other arts. The point would be to excite that older person into mentally participating in today's society. Then the young people would see to it that their 'grandparents' exercise or get to a Preventive Care class, take walks, become involved in worthwhile projects once again. Life is only meaningful if we are needed, loved and involved. The youth of this country can literally 'turn on' its old people."

Preventive Care make no mistake, is a revolution. For decades people have been told to take it easy, slow down, baby themselves. Now along comes Frankel and others like him and say it's time to wake up the body, increase its endurance, work at being fit. They are saying the body is good for a lot more years than most people get from it. The unique feature of the Frankel Foundation's program is that there is something in it for everybody. It's body ecology. They are truly recycling the old into the new. Not even the lame, the diseased, the chronically ill, are overlooked. There is help even for them to reverse the ravages of disease and unchecked aging. For all of those it will bring preventive medicine into their lives, and allow them to slow aging by enhancing health and creating self-esteem.

When the new headquarters for Preventive Care is ready in Charleston, and hundreds of "missionaries" are chosen from rank-and-file Americans over fifty who want to help their peer group, and television acts as a display window to show what Preventive Care can do, then what?

America will be in for a new age where all of its citizens are active and productive. Dr. Raymond Harris, president of the Center for the Study of Aging in Albany, sums it up for us when he says, "Lawrence Frankel has really set off an explosion that should reverberate around the world and promote better physical fitness among older people."

All of you can help, too. Today hundreds are writing their congressmen and senators, urging them to read this book on the Preventive Care Revolution and then vote for funds to bring its concepts and practice to all Americans.

But if our Government continues to ignore mass aging research programs, many adults living today—you and I included—will be deprived of the possibility of achieving a vigorous old age.

By expressing your concern in letters to congress now, urging money for all types of research into aging and for Preventive Care's "now" program, you'll help yourself and your family. Past history proves that financial support on a nationwide Government basis is always in direct relationship to the demands voters and taxpayers make for appropriations.

Interest in Preventive Care is mounting. Frankel gained recruits when he wrote a weekly column, "Fitness is Ageless" in the *Charleston Daily Mail*. And a new book now is being prepared on the First Appalachian Conference of Physical Activity and Aging, sponsored by the Frankel Foundation in 1973, that will be edited by Dr. Harris and Frankel and published by Charles Thomas and Sons. It will be directed toward the medical community and to professionals involved in the study of gerontology, and will urge medical support for Preventive Care.

My first national article on Preventive Care, which appeared in the April-May issue, 1973, of *Modern Maturity* magazine, and was read by the six million subscribers of its parent organization, The American Association of Retired People, deluged both Frankel and myself with mail from Americans wanting details on how to start such a program in their own homes—now. This book is dedicated to those who wrote us.

Frankel will continue to address medical conventions, societies, conferences for older Americans, and Government agencies to further spread Preventive Care's message. When he and Dr. Carl Roncaglione gave their paper on Preventive Care at the twentieth Olympiad's International Congress on Sports, Medicine, and Physical Fitness in Munich, Germany, in 1972, they made powerful friends. Doctors and gerontology specialists from all over the world wanted to know more. Some countries, as a result, already are far ahead of ours in implementing this plan for the elderly.

Dr. Paul Dudley White, the famed heart specialist who attended President Dwight D. Eisenhower, reinforced Preventive Care's importance in a letter to Frankel. He said, "There are large numbers of the elderly who might never consent to enter into formalized programs, but who nonetheless need to be convinced that they must use their muscles and their minds. Therefore we should assemble those who would adopt a missionary approach toward reaching those large numbers who are rapidly declining toward total immobility."

Medicine in the United States has largely overlooked the role of preventive medicine and the importance of motivation. This inscription, at the burial place of poet John Dryden, 1631-1700, observed by Frankel, says it all:

> By chase, our long lived fathers earned their feed,
> Toil strung the nerves and purified the blood;
> But we, their sons, a pampered race of men,
> Are dwindled down to three score years and ten.
> Better to use your muscles, for health unbought,
> Then fee the doctors for a nauseous draught.
> The wise, for cure, on exercise depend,
> God never made his work for man to mend.

The time is ripe now for Preventive Care. It is the wave of the future.

One of the joys of Preventive Care classes is the friendship and fun generated through meetings. At the finish of each class, the group joins in a dance circle for their final routine.

Chapter 18

Begin Your New Life-Style—Preventive Care

WHEN THE MOTION-PICTURE industry honored actor James Cagney in a television special in March of 1974, fans noticed with delight the zany little dance step Jimmy did as he ascended the stage. Still the peppery and beguiling little Irishman at seventy-five he was in his youth, reporters asked him "How come you are so fit?"

"Exercise," explained Jimmy. "Try to get out of breath twice a day. Never take your heart by surprise." The movie great, who retired thirteen years ago to a farm in upstate New York, admitted he gets up at 5.30 A.M., does little tap dance step and jogs in place to dance music each morning.

Norman Rockwell, enjoying now at eighty a revival of his illustrative art in everything from books to ceramics, works seven days a week—and is a bicycle nut. When weather permits, the famous Saturday Evening Post illustrator and his wife, Molly, bicycle near his home in Stockbridge, Massachusetts. "In the summertime we go every day. We never miss it. I want to be working on a picture and just fall over, dead. That's my ideal. I don't want to sit in a chair, or go to Florida, or anything like that." Rockwell says the only way of life for him is an active one.

And then there's Emma White Hudson, of Marco Island, Florida, a fragile-looking ninety-two-year-old grandmother who keeps fit by rowing her twelve-foot boat along the Gulf Coast almost daily. She says of her exercise plan, "I love to fish because it helps me sleep better." The ninety-pound nonagenarian uses oars to propel herself to where the fish are biting. She lives alone.

And remember the famous Larry Lewis, the walker who

143

astounded doctors for years with his seven-mile jogs around Golden Gate Park in San Francisco? He died at 106. When he was 105 he retired as a full-time waiter and took a part-time job as good-will ambassador for Western Girl, Inc., a temporary-help agency, because "I was bored."

All of these people found living to their fullest meant a viable old age, full of challenge and personal satisfaction.

There is no reason why you who are reading this book can't emulate any one of them. First of all you will need a change of attitude toward exercise.

"But how can I exercise now," many of you might say, "when I never have before?" We've shown you in the chapters preceding this that whether or not you've exercised before doesn't matter. Now you must decide you want to live a full, independent life into your old age.

A Catholic priest and author, Father Gerald Hoenig, once said: "*You* can change the world. It's very simple; you just start by changing yourself, so that you live the way you would like the world to live. The world then already will have begun to change."

Then, after you decide exercise will become a part of your new life-style, you will need the blessing of your doctor to begin. If you live in a remote rural area where medical advice isn't handy except in emergencies, seek out the aid of the visiting nurses Association or the public-health agency in your community. Show them this book and its exercises to determine what, if any, limitations you must impose on yourself.

Once you have medical consent to begin, remember you didn't get flabby and inactive all in one day so you can't grow firm and fit over a weekend. Do this Preventive Care program in steps, starting with simple low-mobility exercises contained in Chapter 20. Work at the lowest level for each exercise you do and gradually increase, when your endurance increases, to the maximum number of times recommended for each routine.

But before you begin, a word about music. We've shown in all the plans of Preventive Care in action today that music enhances both mood and tolerance. That means you should find either records or cassette tapes of music that has a definite beat and makes you want to move about.

In Charleston Betty Richard has favorites she uses in the Preventive Care classes there. They are not the only ones, by far. But for guidelines only, here are the ones they like:

1. *André Kostelanetz' Greatest Hits* (Columbia Stereo 9740)
2. *Strauss Waltzes* (Columbia Stereo 8162)
3. *Boston Pops Varieties* (Reader's Digest Records—RDA 98-04)
4. *Reader's Digest Mood Music Album* (Reader's Digest Records—RDA 141-04)
5. Montovani and Orchestra: *Strauss Waltzes Album* (London PS118-Decca)
6. André Kostelanetz: *Concert in the Park* (Columbia Stereo 9488)
7. *Lawrence Welk Presents Myron Floren's New Sound* (Ranwood Records—RLP 8005)
8. Herb Alpert's Tijuana Brass: *Whipped Cream and Other Delights* (A & M Records—SP 4110)
9. Ray Anthony's "Bunny Hop" (45 rpm) (Capitol 6026)

There are many musical exercise albums on the market. But you do not want those that have vocal exercise regimens incorporated into the music as some of them are too strenuous for use in a Preventive Care program. What you seek is just the music you like to make exercise a pleasant way to start a day.

Next you must plan your exercise program at a special time of day, every day. It is important that you remain consistent. The best way to make this program of Preventive Care part of your new life-style is to pick a time, say 9 A.M. each morning, or whenever you awaken, as "your time of day." Allow no one to interfere. Consider it as important as bathing and grooming.

Doing Preventive Care exercises in the morning as a routine after waking insures you that it will in a short time become habit, something you can't do without. Of course, you can incorporate it into any part of the day that suits your personal way of life, but it should be at a time that insures continuity.

Many think about exercise but procrastinate about getting started themselves or assisting others to do it. Dr. Paul Bergevin, Ph.D., writing in *Education* magazine, said: "Too many of us are apathetic and unconcerned about the common person. 'Let the other fellow take care of himself; that's what I have to do,' is not the valid cry of democracy. A citizen must know and act intelligently on what he knows or somebody will act for him.

"Nature abhors a vacuum; in social as in physical vacuums, something will try to fill the gap. Someone will always come to the fore to tell us what to do and how and when to do it, and to take from us the burden of thinking and responsibility; only to replace it with one of submission."

And for those of us growing old, that means going into nursing homes for custodial care and often only because we fail to act for ourselves and loved ones before it is too late.

Now is the time to add quality to your life through Preventive Care. You have the exercises in the book to start. After you have mastered them, and have greater endurance, you might want to consider joining a group to do Preventive Care routines together, say three times a week. If you do, you can work with centers for seniors in your community to get organized. For additional material, and assistance in getting started, you can write directly to the Frankel Foundation, Virginia & Brooks Streets, Charleston, West Virginia 25301, for the latest available material and—encouragement.

Dr. John L. Boyer, a San Diego, California physician who is one of the fourteen appointees to the President's Council of Physical Fitness and Sports, urges Americans to exercise, but with caution. He said that the over-forty set who plans to do strenuous exercise, say on a weekend, and is not prepared for it, is courting disaster. "The weekender suddenly stresses himself and puts a great demand on his heart, not knowing whether or not it can take it."

That's why we urge you to talk with your physician about what exercise you can do now, and later on. The reason Preventive Care exercises are so important to your health is that they are designed to improve your cardio-vascular system. After fifty or so you don't need big muscles, you need exercise to help your heart and lungs perform at maximum efficiency.

Remember the stunt Frankel performed when he turned forty to prove to his YMCA youth group that calendar age is no indication of strength? Well, when he was sixty-one he did it again. He climbed nineteen flights of stairs wearing a harness equipped with one-hundred pounds of weights. Frankel made the climb to show that older people could develop ample cardio-vascular reserve by a program of systematic exercise. Both his pulse and blood pressure were checked by a doctor and were in the normal range at the end of the climb.

Frankel, now in his seventieth year, continues to exercise, to the constant amazement of his peers and the youth of his community. Mention to him the story of the Boy or Girl Scout helping the "little old lady across the street" and you'll incite his ire. He hates that image of helplessness.

"If a youngster ever did that to me I'd probably pick him up and *carry* him across to show that we older people not only have mobility, but real strength. It doesn't have to diminish with age."

After you begin to feel stronger and more alert, it's time to extend your exercise program to include more "fun" activities that also are good for that cardio-vascular system.

What are they? Brisk walking. That's something anyone can do. Climbing stairs. Bicycle riding, swimming, and if your doctor approves, jogging. Golf, the experts feel, is a nice recreation but it's not good "heart" exercise.

Dr. Paul Dudley White, who corresponded with Frankel and encouraged him to spread Preventive Care to seniors in America, told the following story in a report in *The New York Times Magazine:* (June 23, 1957).

"An aged friend and patient of mine had the flu in midwinter and was confined to the house for several months. While he sat about, both legs began to swell. When I saw him in early spring he was discouraged and apprehensive."

"Examination showed that his heart was not responsible, nor any actual thrombosis (clotting), but simply a sluggish circulation and the effect of gravity in an aged person. Instead of medicine, the resumption of his regular exercise of walking, up to a mile or two a day, was prescribed and within ten days the leg swelling disappeared. Now, three years later, he continues to be in excellent health."

When man feels good, it stimulates his mental abilities, too, a bonus of the Preventive Care program. Dr. White believed in mental stimulation also.

Workers who have mental jobs need exercise to keep their

minds clear. "Mental concentration should be alternated with exercise or even accompanied by it, as was the custom of peripatetic philosophers of ancient Greece," said Dr. White.

There is today an old people's "lib" movement. In Philadelphia in the fall of 1972, at a pre-election speech of then Vice President Spiro Agnew, the men of the Secret Service encountered "Gray Panthers," a group of about two-hundred militant old people who were protesting the Administration's social-service budget cuts. A sixty-seven-year-old woman named Margaret Kuhn dashed toward a young guard and announced, "Zap, you're getting old! Listen to what we are saying. We're trying to change things for you."

While not all of us with gray in our hair want to demonstrate to bring about a change in the attitudes of the nation towards its aging population, we want to stay informed. One of the militants' strongest stands calls for the abolishment of "compulsory retirement." They maintain that if you are productive on the job at sixty-four, your sixty-fifth birthday doesn't change anything.

And we all are going to live longer. Already there are scientists seeking the key to a two-hundred year life span. A Michigan State University research team announced in March of 1974 they may have discovered a drug that might lead to prolonged human life—possibly even to two-hundred years. The drug would "switch off the human thermostat" so that the body temperature could be lowered and the aging process slowed dramatically. They added that perhaps in ten years, if their tests prove successful, they'd be ready to try this drug on humans.

But what about the quality of life? That's where Preventive Care comes in. If you are vibrant and alert, you'll want to live as long as possible. But without a combined physical and mental posture of good health, what's the use?

"Our decade is witnessing the rise of a whole new generation of elders," the Panthers' Ms. Kuhn said. "We live longer, we're more vigorous physically. We're better educated and more articulate. And consciousness-raising has made us aware of how our society puts us down."

You, as one individual, can reverse that role society has cast for you by now pledging to yourself a life pattern designed to keep both your body and mind alive.

Paul Trounier, in *Learn To Grow Old* (Harper and Row, 1972) cited the compensations of aging when he said: "All the renuncistims demanded by old age are in the field of action, not in that of the heart and mind. They belong to the order of 'doing,' not that of 'being.' I live differently, but not less. Life is different, but it is still fully life—even fuller, if that were possible. My interest and participating in the world is not diminishing, but increasing.

"In a well-known declaration, general Douglas MacArthur said, in 1945: 'You don't get old from living a particular number of years; you get old because you have deserted your ideals. Years wrinkle your skin, renouncing your ideals wrinkles your soul. Worry, doubt, fear, and despair are all enemies which slowly bring us down to the ground and turn us to dust before we die.'

"You can still live intensely as you advance in years. If there is a 'minus' there is also a 'plus,' and it is the 'plus' of my old age which gives it its meaning and which I must now try to define. One loses something only in order to acquire something else. There is something to discover in old age, an aspect of life which could not be known before."

Which means, for you and for me, staying physically and mentally alive all of our years. It means caring for what happens to others. It means liking yourself first, and once confident in that posture, liking others. It means letting go of your adult children, yet maintaining such a full life of your own that they will want to come back, time and again, to see what that "spry mother and dad" are up to. It means being able to live and cope in this age of stress with mental and physical ease, because your body and mind are in tune. Then when "shock waves" come, they'll bounce off of you.

Now to the exercises. You have your doctor's permission, you have the routines all illustrated for you, you have music to exercise by. You have a set time of day to do them. Now let's get started.

At the Frankel Foundation in Charleston, West Virginia, citizens of all ages, from middle age to the mid-nineties, work out in one of the three gymnasiums. Passing the medicine ball around is one of the exercises. Instructor is Betty Richard, center.

Chapter 19

Preventive Care Exercises

HERE THEY ARE—low-mobility exercises you can perform daily in your own home no matter where you live, or how limited you are physically or financially.

Ponce de León sought for years a fountain of youth. You have one right in your broom closet, because in it there is a household broom that will now become part of your exercise equipment. For Preventive Care's regimens you'll need to cut off a fourteen-inch section from any old broom, or if you have only a working one, you can go to any hardware store and ask them to cut you a stick to size.

Now, unless you have wall-to-wall carpeting in the room where you plan to exercise, you'll need a mat or an old piece of carpet large enough to allow you to stretch out on.

Finally, you'll want to have two two-pound dumbbells, which you can purchase quite reasonably in any store that sells sporting goods. If you'd prefer, you can substitute two unopened cans of vegetables, each weighing one pound.

That's it. That is all of the equipment you'll need to start your Preventive Care exercises.

Now pick a time of day you can set aside to do your regimen daily. As we indicated earlier, it can be right after you wake up, or later on, depending entirely on your own schedule. The most important thing is that you select a time that truly is convenient for you, a time that fits into your day so well you won't be tempted to find excuses to postpone or ignore it.

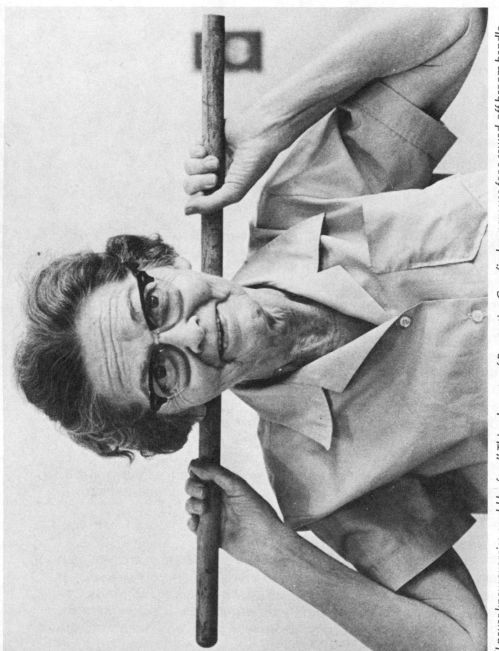

"I never knew exercise could be fun." This advocate of Preventive Care finds a new use for a sawed-off broom handle.

Many people who have adopted Preventive Care exercises as their new life-style have found that doing them in the afternoon or even later in the day doesn't work out too well. Often as the day lengthens, you find you are getting tired, and then you are more reluctant to stick to your regimen.

Mornings seem best for most people. Preventive Care exercises done early in the day then can become a part of your living routine quite easily, like combing your hair, showering, or brushing your teeth.

In time these exercises will become so much of a habit that you'll feel deprived if something, like an illness, prevents you from doing them, even for a brief time. Do remember, even if you are confined to your bed, you can still exercise. Remember Myrtle Bloom in Chapter 10, who was hospitalized with a severe attack of arthritis. She wouldn't quit, not even then. Instead, she wiggled her feet and hands, keeping her limbs as flexible as possible until she could do more. It speeded up her full recovery, both mentally as well as physically.

These exercises will strengthen your muscles and increase your flexibility, and in so doing will cut down on the likelihood of having accidents or falls

So, first obtain your doctor's permission to start these low-mobility exercises illustrated in the pages to follow, then assemble your equipment in a special room of the house where you'll be exercising, and decide on a definite hour of the day when you'll begin. Then—go.

You'll never regret it. Body ecology works. You'll be recycling your old body for a new one. And the benefits will last you all of the days of your life.

1. STRETCHING EXERCISES
to improve flexibility of the spinal column

1A—Sitting in erect position, hands on knees, bend slowly forward at waist, keeping head between arms and reach as far as possible. Knees must be held flat to floor. Hold position to count of ten. Repeat twice. (This first exercise is especially good for improving the flexibility of the lower back and hamstrings.)

1B-1—*Same starting position as #1A. Bring forehead as close as possible to the knee, holding on to calf, ankle or toes (depending on your beginning flexibility). Hold to count of ten. Repeat twice, on right and left sides.*

1B-2 and 1B-3—Photographs showing varying degrees of flexibility of exercise #1B-1.

1C—*Same starting position as #1A. Bring legs together, knees flat to floor. Bend gently forward at waist, keeping head between arms, reach as far forward as possible, holding position at either knees, calves, ankles, or toes. (You should be able to reach farther week by week). Hold to S-L-O-W count of twenty. Start out by doing three repetitions of this exercise and work up to ten repetitions.*

2. NECK EXERCISES

to improve the function and flexibility of the neck

2A and 2A-1—Neck Circles. *In sitting position, rotate head S-L-O-W-L-Y to the right, making large complete circles, ten times.*

Reverse circles to the left S-L-O-W-L-Y ten times.

3. SHOULDER EXERCISES
to improve flexibility of the shoulders

3A—Shoulder Shrugs. *Arms at sides, shrug shoulders up toward the ears ten times.*

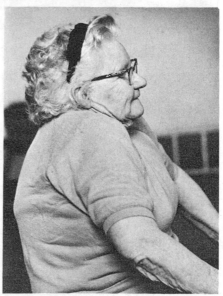

3B—Shoulder Rotations. *Shrug and rotate shoulders forward, slowly, five times. Shrug and rotate shoulders backward five times.*

4. ARM CIRCLES
to improve posture and flexibility of the shoulders

Extend arms horizontally sidewards, head held in good posture, with palms down. Rotate arms from the shoulders, making very small circles, ten times forward and then reverse.

5. HAND ROTATION
to improve flexibility of the wrist

Grasp right wrist with left hand. S-L-O-W-L-Y rotate right hand, keeping palm facing down, ten times clockwise and then rotate hand counter-clockwise ten times. Repeat same procedure with opposite hand.

6. FINGER EXERCISES
to improve flexibility of the fingers

6A-1 and 6A-2—Finger Stretch. With palm of right hand facing down, gently force fingers back toward forearm, using left hand for leverage; then place left hand on top of right hand and force fingers down. Repeat five times, each hand.

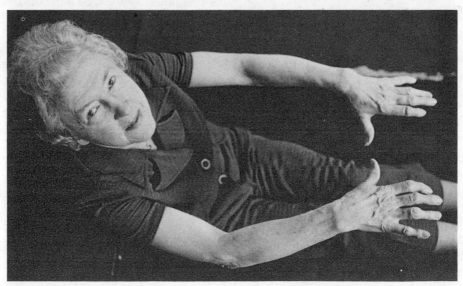

6B-1 and 6B-2—Finger Flexion and Extension. *Arms extended forward, close fist tightly, then extend fingers. Flex and extend ten times.*

7. ANKLE EXERCISES

to improve flexibility of the ankles

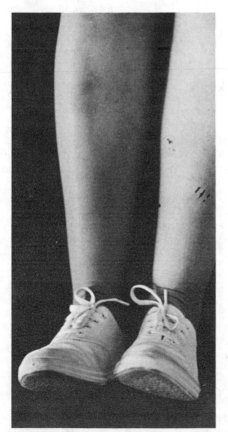 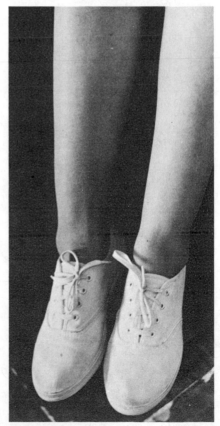

7B-1 and 7B-2—Ankle Flexion and Extension. *With legs extended, stretch ankles forward, then backward. Flex and extend ten times.*

8. THIGH ABDUCTORS AND ADDUCTORS
to firm muscles inside and outside the thighs

8A—From sitting position (floor, chair, or couch): Start with knees together, hands on outside, separate knees against resistance of hands to slow count of five.

8B—With knees separated, hands inside, bring knees together to slow count of five against hand resistance. Repeat this exercise five times each direction.

9. RAG DOLL EXERCISE
to relax the lower back and stretch the hamstrings

Perform in standing position, legs approximately twelve inches apart. Bend forward at waist, head remaining between arms, bounce gently toward the floor, chin toward chest. Reach as far as possible without forcing the movement and then return to standing position. Repeat exercise four times.

   Important note: Throughout the entire exercise the head remains between the arms and the knees should not be bent.

10. LYING-ON-BACK EXERCISES

10A—Flexibility Exercise—to stretch the hamstrings. *From lying-on-back position, legs fully extended, arms at side, swing right leg up and backward as far as possible and return ten times. Repeat ten times with left leg.*

10B—Back Relaxation—for the lower back. *From lying-on-back position, grasp right knee with both hands and pull toward chest, at the same time bring chin toward the knee. Do three times. Repeat with other knee three times. Do this exercise three times, adding one repetition each week until you can do ten comfortably.*

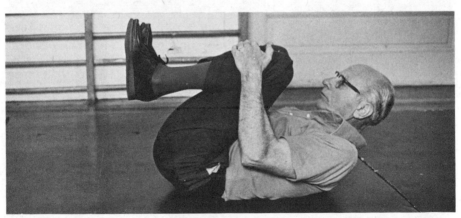

10C—Same as 10B, except grasp both knees and bring to chest as closely as possible, bringing chin toward knee. Do three times, adding one repetition each week until you can do ten.

11. HALF-SIT-UPS
to strengthen the upper abdominal muscles

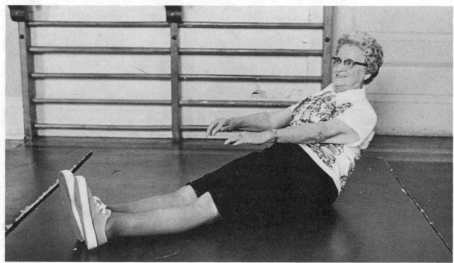

From position lying on back, legs extended, arms behind head, reach up and forward to touch fingers to beginning of knee caps. Hold this position for count of three and return to starting position. Important: Exhale forcefully with the effort—never hold the breath. *Start with no more than three repetitions, gradually increasing by one each week to a maximum of ten.* 11-1—*Photograph shows the starting position of the half-sit-up.*

11-2—*Photograph shows the half-sit-up completed to the correct position.*

12. BACK ARCH SUPPORT

firms the back of the arms and strengthens the upper back muscles

12-1—Start from sitting position, upper body erect, hands behind and slightly to the side.

12-2—Raise hips from floor until body is perfectly straight with head back and hold for count of three. Return to starting position and repeat exercise three times. Increase one repetition each week until you can perform a maximum of ten.

13. THIGH AND HIP EXERCISES

to strengthen and improve the flexibility of the
thighs, hips, and the muscles at the sides of your waist

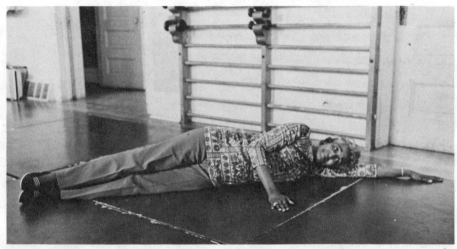

13—From lying-on-side position, one arm fully extended, other arm to the side in front of waist for balance, back slightly arched:

13A—Raise leg up as far as possible, but do not bend the knee and point toes. Repeat three times.

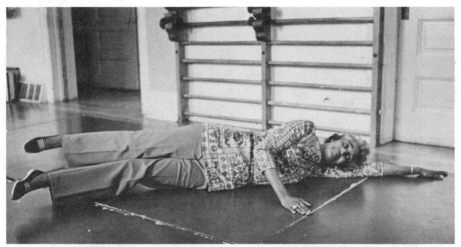

13B—*Kick legs in scissor fashion, fast cadence, ten times.*

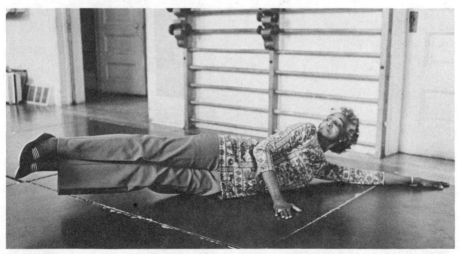

13C—*Raise both legs and upper body simultaneously, looking over shoulder toward heels, three times. Repeat these exercises lying on other side.*

14. POSTURE EXERCISES
to improve flexibility of the shoulder girdle muscles

14A—Start in sitting position, alternately raise the two-pound dumbbells to shoulder level, hands passing each other. Count one—and—two—and—etc. Perform a minimum of five times. Optimum ten times.

Instead of dumbbells, you may use portion of broomstick, raising from knees to shoulder level. A one-pound can of vegetables in each hand is also a good substitute for the dumbbells.

14B—Start in sitting position, upper body erect, 2-pound dumbbells resting on knees. Raise dumbbells forward and upward to vertical position, arms always perfectly straight. Stretch so that inside of arms are close to ears. Do at least five times. Optimum ten times. (This exercise may be done using two one-pound cans of vegetables or with a 14-inch portion of a broomstick.)

14C. POSTURE EXERCISES
to improve flexibility of the extensors of the wrists and upper arm

14C-1—Using two-pound dumbbells or two one-pound cans of vegetables, punch alternately forward and backward so hands pass each other a minimum of five times.

14C-2—Using broomstick, in place of dumbbells, hold firmly to chest, push forward vigorously and back to chest a minimum of five times. Optimum ten times.

14D. POSTURE EXERCISES

to improve flexibility of the shoulder girdle and the extensors of the wrists

14D—Arm Circles. *Arms extended horizontally sideward, stretch hard. Make small concentric circles. Circle forward five times and then backward five times. Use two-pound dumbbells or two one-pound cans of vegetables.*

14E—Sema-phore—to improve flexibility of the shoulder-girdle and the extensors of the wrists. Stretch one arm vertically close to ear, other arm horizontal sideward, palm up. Using two-pound dumbbells or two one-pound cans of vegetables, alternately shift the sema-phore position left to right, and right to left. Perform a minimum of five times. The optimum is ten repetitions.

14F and G. BROOMSTICK DRILLS
to improve flexibility of the shoulders and the upper spine

14F—From sitting position with 14-inch broomstick resting on knees, raise broomstick forward and upward behind neck, then return to starting position. Repeat five times.

14G—Start by placing a 14-inch broomstick behind neck as illustrated in picture then twist entire trunk from the waist as far as possible to the right and then as far as possible to the left. Maintain erect position of the head.

Note: The posture exercise series should start with a minimum of five repetitions, increasing each week until you can easily do twenty.

15. QUADRAPEDAL SERIES—CAT EXERCISES
to improve tone of abdominal muscles and to improve posture

15A-1 and 15A-2—As in illustration, support weight on hands and knees, keeping arms straight and head up. Lower head toward chest, then S-L-O-W-L-Y pull stomach muscles toward backbone to count of five (humping back like a cat), hold to count of five, then relax to original starting position. Repeat this exercise five times.

From starting position on hands and knees—
15B-1—Lower head toward chest, S-L-O-W-L-Y bring right knee toward chin.

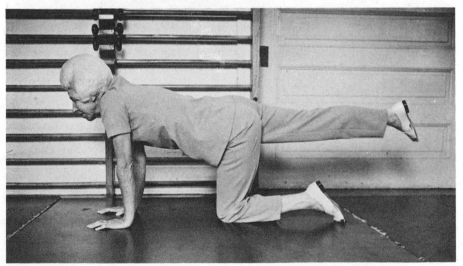

15B-2—Then extend right leg backward and raise head.

15B-3—Extend left arm forward and upward—this final position is called scale. Alternate five times each side. (This second exercise is especially good for strengthening the back and improving the sense of balance.)

16. LEG LUNGING
to firm the muscles of the thighs and derriere

In a standing position, place hands on hips and put feet together. Lunge forward, back leg straight (upper body should always be vertical, do not lean forward). Return to starting position.
Lunge as follows: Forward and backward, right leg. Then forward and backward, left leg. Repetitions. Do a minimum of five and an optimum of twenty for each leg.

17. EXTERNAL OBLIQUE

to improve the flexibility of and to strengthen the sides of the waist

Standing in erect position, legs together, arms at side, step to the right side with the right arms circling over head, leaning body toward the left. Return to erect position and repeat opposite side. Repeat a minimum of five times and an optimum of ten for each side.

18 HYPEREXTENSIONS

to strengthen the upper and lower back

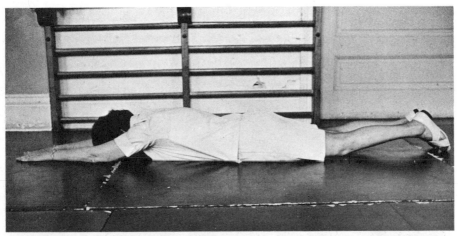

18-1—Start from front lying position with arms and legs fully extended and head down.

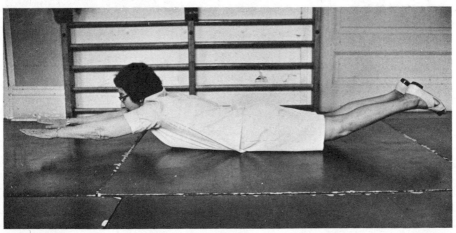

18-2—Raise arms, legs, and head simultaneously, arching the entire body without bending arms and legs.

18-3—Maintaining this same arch position, extend arms sideward, then extend arms forward, holding momentarily, and return to starting position. This is a four-count exercise and should be repeated three times; later increase repetitions by one each week to a maximum of ten.

19. HALF KNEE BENDS
to firm muscles of the thighs and derriere

Stand with heels together, toes pointed out. Back must be perfectly straight. Squat to half knee bend, keeping hands on hips. Start out by doing five repetitions and work up to ten.

Epilogue

By Dr. Raymond Harris, M.D.

(Clinical Assistant Professor of Medicine, Albany Medical College; author, *The Management of Geriatric Cardiovascular Disease;* (J.B. Lippincott Company, 1970); Editor of *The Gerontologist;* President, The Center for the Study of Aging, Inc.)

OLDER PEOPLE DON'T exercise because they are stereotyped, fashioned by a "society" that says they shouldn't. As a result, too many withdraw from physical activities, do not exercise because of that stereotype, and thereby accelerate their aging changes and physical deterioration.

I do not know for certain that physical activity always increases longevity, but it does add greatly to the enjoyment of life. We must motivate elderly people to be more active and to resist the ravages and unhappiness of old age.

One should not only pay attention to his body but should also exercise his mind, because to be really healthy and fit there is an equal need for intellectual activity. A fit person is one who is physically and mentally alert and never falls into the insidious "senior citizen" mold cast by old-fashioned societal and cultural patterns.

Make no mistake: Physical activity does help one resist the reversible impairments of old age and all its consequent ailments and complaints. By becoming active and independent now, the near-to-retirement or retired person can discard senior citizenship in favor of first-class citizenship forevermore.

Appendix I

THE FOLLOWING IS a sample copy of the consent-letter used by the Lawrence Frankel Foundation for its Preventive Care classes in Charleston, West Virginia. It can be modified by any group that wants to start Preventive Care classes in their own city. The letters should be filed along with other important data collected on each individual participant as the class progresses.

DATE _____

Dear _____ :

My patient _____ may participate in the specially designed low-level program for seniors with the type of supervision approved by the Frankel Foundation's Medical Advisory Committee.

I understand that the program for the foundation's project of Preventive Care has been read and approved by the Kanawha Medical Society.

(Doctor--Please note at the bottom of this form if there are any contraindications or special instructions. Also indicate what, if any, medication the patient is now taking.)

Age of patient _____ Weight _____ Height _____

Smoking habits _____

Home telephone number of patient _____

Patient's home address _____

Appendix II

THE FOLLOWING IS the award certificate the University of IOWA gives to its seniors who participate regularly in one of its programs of physical fitness at Iowa City retirement centers and nursing homes. The co-leaders in these programs, Dr. David K. Leslie and Dr. John W. McLure, feel such a certificate helps. Everyone likes to be "rewarded" for his efforts. In the Preventive Care classes in Charleston, Lawrence Frankel, too, honors participants with small trophies attesting to their fitness sucess.

Hawkeye (University's Mascot) Physical Fitness Award

In the 20th century, no nation or individual should yield to physical or spiritual waste. A few minutes regularly invested in physical exercise will yield hours of improved living. The spectator endures life; the participant enhances it.

This achievement award certifies that _____
has demonstrated personal leadership by participating in a physical fitness program in cooperation with the University of Iowa.

Signed _____

Title _____

Date _____

Appendix III

THE FOLLOWING IS a speech presented by Lawrence Frankel at the Institute On Man and Science, Rensselaerville, New York, on September 21, 1973, during its "Fitness After Fifty" Seminar. It is printed here to sum up Preventive Care founder's philosophy on why fitness is so important for maturing Americans.

Maximizing Fitness Motivation for the Elderly
Lawrence Frankel

> King Solomon and King David
>> Led merry, merry lives
> They had many, many lady friends
>> And many, many wives.
>
> But when old age crept over them
>> With many, many qualms
> King Solomon wrote the Proverbs
>> And King David wrote the Psalms.

How can we delay old age?
How can we prolong youth?

The ancient alchemists searched for a mysterious substance capable of transmuting baser metals to gold or silver and that would, in addition, *prolong life*. The more current search for the elixir of youth resides in the ivory towers of multitudes of researchers in gerontology and geriatrics.

How far have we *really* advanced with numerous symposia and thousands of imposing dissertations? With better than twenty million elderly Americans, more than half living at or below the poverty level, how long must we await pragmatic, down-to-earth intervention in our mass human obsolescence?

Poor, old King David, in desperation, tired "geronomic," the ancient belief that inhaling the breath of young women restored virility, as attested to in Kings 1: 1-4, wherein Abishag the Shunamite, a sixteen-year-old virgin was brought to his bed to keep him warm. The Bible relates that he knew her not, and died soon thereafter.

A prestigious midwestern university involved in aging research and bio-medical studies, in one of their flyers, suggested for recommended reading a best seller, dealing with the search of the so-called beautiful people for eternal youth, their "miracle doctors" and how they helped them retain or revive their looks and energies. Some of the names are quite well-known—Jackie Kennedy Onassis, Ginger Rogers, Frank Sinatra, Eddie Fisher, Marilyn Monroe, and a host of others, *ad nauseam!*

A recent nationwide sixty-minute televised program showed numerous vignettes of these too-rich, fashionable devotees of rejuvenation being injected in their flaccid derièrres. The wan hopeful smiles in wrinkled countenances was a sad commentary. Have we come full circle from King David's geronomic? Would the use of millions of young Abishags (if they could be found), be a better way to find Nirvana?

It is strange that the so-called "beautiful people" are considered real news, while our millions of elderly cast aside are worthy of discussion only at symposia, seminars, White House conferences, etc.

In *our* nation, more so than in most nations, giving in to old age has become a socially accepted behavior pattern, as evidenced by proliferating growth of nursing homes, spiraling numbers in hospitals and extended care facilities, and vast multitudes supported by Government welfare. With more than half our aging living near or below the poverty level, insufficient Medicare can literally mean Medi-*scare* and Medicaid, *too little aid.*

The yet untried method in dealing with the problems of our aging population is that of *prevention*—the inhibiting and decelerating of the degenerative hypokinetic processes inherent in enforced sedentary lives of our elderly.

We would humbly suggest for consideration, such programs as our action-oriented Preventive Care. We base this in part on the experiences of our initial pilot project and on our current "demonstration" with several groups—divers in character and background, with varying degrees of mobility and immobility—whose lifestyle had precluded *ever* any involvement in sport, recreation, or supervised physical activity.

It had been a privilege to observe the many who initially appeared hopeless and dispirited *undergo* real metamorphosis, physically, emotionally, and mentally!

Inactivity quite often leads to immobility, the precursor to institutionalization, often in substandard facilities which strike terror in the hearts of many of our aging.

There is an urgent need for *mass motivation* to involve millions of our elderly in stimulating mental and physical life-styles.

A floodgate of correspondence concerning "Project Preventive Care" followed shortly after the March, 1973, symposium on Physical Activity and Aging. The stage demonstration of divers groups included the lame, the halt, and the blind in a real heterogeneous mixture of ambulatory and nonambulatory individuals. All represented groups seldom invited to participate in formal exercise programs—most came to classes initially with a self-image of hopelessness and a sense of rejection. If we reflect the expressed opinions of the panel of distinguished observers who critiqued the staged demonstration—"they saw what was almost unbelievable and unique"—yet it was but a simple response to a common denominator of love and concern.

A month following the seminar, a story concerning *these subjects* appeared in a nationally prominent publication subscribed to by the *retired,* and ever since increasing numbers of letters from almost every state in the nation, with pleas and supplications for help and suggestions for initiating similar programs, arrive almost daily. These strongly reinforce our belief that a tremendous void and need exists, to which we must address ourselves—and soon.

Can we re-motivate to active physical and mental life patterns, the millions of sedentary, inactive, dispirited, and often despairing from among our aging populations? Can we give new hope to the lame, the halt, the blind—those in wheelchairs and walkers?

May we present to you, in lieu of numerous graphs, charts, and statistical corroborations, the "nuts and bolts" approach, as Dr. Harris characterized it, of exciting dramatic *living-color* case histories from among as charming a group of "young oldsters" as you would search far and wide to find on our nation! (A slide presentation follows.)

Bibliography

Andersen, K. Lange, M.D. *Fundamentals of Exercise Testing.* World Health Organization, Geneva, Switzerland.

Annals of the New York Academy of Sciences. *Body Composition.* Published by the Academy.

Annals of the New York Academy of Sciences. Vol. 131, Art. 1, Published by the Academy.

Aronson, Charles N. *Regimen.* Charles N. Aronson Book Publisher RRI, Arcade, N.Y. 14009, 1973.

Astrand, Per-Olaf. *Experimental Studies of Physical Working Capacity in Relation to Sex and Age.* Dept. of Physiology. Kungliga. Gymnastiska Centralinsitutet: Stockholm.

Astrand, Per-Olaf and Kaare Rodahl. *Textbook of Work Physiology.* McGraw-Hill Book Company.

Audio Cassettes, First Appalachian Conference on Physical Activity and Aging, March 2-4, 1973, Frankel Foundation, Virginia at Brooks, Charleston, W.Va. 25301.

Kretschmer, Ernst, Dr. *Korperbau Und Charakter.* Berlin, Verlag Von Julius Springer, 1936.

Best, Charles Herbert, C.B.E., M.A., M.D., D. Sc. and Taylor, Norman Burke, V.D., M.D., F.R.S. *The Physiological Basis of Medical Practice.* Publisher, The Williams and Wilkins Company.

Bierman, William, M.D. and Licht, Sidney, M.D. *Physical Medicine in General Practice.* A Hoeber-Harper Book.

Blackeslee, Alton and Stamler, Jeremiah, M.D. *Your Heart Has Nine Lives.* Prentice-Hall, Inc.

Blue Cross, *Generation In The Middle.* Blue Cross Association, 840 North Lake Shore Drive, Chicago, Ill. 60611, 1970.

Blumenfeld, Arthur. *Heart Attack: Are You a Candidate?* Paul S. Eriksson, Inc., N.Y.

Bowen, William Pardon, . . . *Applied Anatomy and Kinesiology.* Lea and Febiger, 1937.

Brams, William A., M.D. *Managing Your Coronary.* J. B. Lippincott.

Brown, Rosco C., Jr. and Kenyson. *Classical Studies On Physical Activity.* Prentice-Hall, Inc.

Bjerre, Poul, M.D. *The History and Practice of Psychanalysis.* The Gorham Press, London, 1916.

Bruch, Hilde, M.D. *The Importance of Overweight.* W. W. Norton and Co., Inc. N.Y., 1957.

Brunner, Daniel, M.D. and Jokl, Ernst, M.D. *Physical Activity and Aging.* S. Karger, Switzerland. Medicine and Sport, Vol. 4.

Buchwald, Edith, M.A., A. P. T. A. *Physical Rehabilitation For Daily Living.* McGraw-Hill Book Co. 1952.

Burger, Robert E. *"Who Cares For the Aged?" Saturday Review,* Jan. 1969.

Cabot, Richard, M.D. *Physical Diagnosis.* William Wood and Co. N.Y. 1927.

Cannon, Walter B., M.D. *Bodily Changes In Pain, Hunger, Fear, and Rage.* Harper and Row, N.Y.

Cannon, Walter B., M.D. *The Wisdom of the Body.* The W. W. Norton Company.

Chaffee, Ellen E., R.N. and Greisheimer, Esther, Ph.D., M.D. *In Basic Physiology and Anatomy.* J. B. Lippincott Co. 1964.

Consolazio, C. Frank. *Physiological Measurements of Metabolic Functions in Man.* McGraw-Hill Book Co., Inc.

Cooper, Kenneth H. *Aerobics.* M. Evans & Co., Inc. with J. B. Lippincott Co., 1968.

Committee on Aging, *Health Aspects of Aging.* Council on Medical Service, American Medical Association 1957.

Crotty, Bryant J. *Movement Behavior and Motor Learning.* Lea and Febiger, Phila. 1964.

Cureton, Thomas Kirk. *Endurance of Young Men.* Society for Research in Child Development. Washington, D.C. National Research Council, 1945.

Cureton, Thomas Kirk. *Physical Fitness Appraisal and Guidance.* The C. V. Mosby Comapny.

Curtin, Sharon R. *Nobody Ever Died of Old Age.* Little-Brown Co.

Dawson, Percy M., M.D. *The Physiology of Physical Education.* Williams and Wilkins Company, 1935.

DE Arte Gymnastica. *Hieronymi Mercurialis.* Published in Venice, 1973.

Deaver, George G., M.D. *Fundamentals of Physical Examination.* W. B. Saunders Co. 1939.

de Beauvoir, Simone. *The Coming of Age.* G. P. Putnam's Sons. 1972.

DE Coubertin, Pierre. *The Olympic Idea.* Germany: Carl-Diem-Institut.

DE Lorme, Thomas L., B.S., M.D. and Watkins, Arthur L., A.B., M.D. *Progressive Resistance Exercise.* Appleton-Century-Crofts, Inc.

De Ropp, Robert S. *Man Against Aging.* St. Martin's Press, N.Y.

Diserens and Fine. *A Psychology of Music.*

Dobbin, E. Virginia. *The Low Fat, Low Cholesterol Diet.* Doubleday and Company, Inc. 1951.

Editors of Prevention Magazine, *How to Live It Up and Live Longer!* Rodale Press, Emmaus, Pa. 18049 1974.

English, O. Spurgeon and Pearson, Gerald H. J. *Common Neuroses of Children and Adults.* W. W. Norton and Company, Inc.

Fleishman, Edwin A. *The Structure and Measurement of Physical Fitness.* Prentice-Hall, Inc.

Forel, August, M.D., Ph.D., L.L.D. Psychotherapy. Allied Publishing Co.

Fox, Samuel III, M.D. and Naughton, John P., M.D. *Physical Activity and the Prevention of Coronary Heart Disease.* From the Divisions of Cardiology and Rehabilitation Medicine.

Frankel, Lawrence J. *Physical Conditioning Program for Asthmatic Children.* Reprinted from the *Journal of the American Medical Association,* December 13, 1958, Vol. 168, pp. 1996-2000.

Frankel, Lawrence J. and Roncaglione, Carl J. M.D. *Physical Fitness for the Aging.* Presented August, 1972 at the Scientific Congress proceeding the 1972 Olympic Games at Munchen, Germany.

Frankel, Lawrence J. and Jokl, Ernst, M.D. *Ergometric Fitness Evaluation of 86 Physicians. American Corrective Therapy Journal,* April, 1968.

Frankel, Lawrence J. and Jokl, Ernst, M.D. "Influence of a Sustained Physical Training Regime on Normo and Hypertensive Middle Aged and Old Men." Published in the *Institute of Occupational Health,* Helsinki, Finland.

Frankel, Lawrence J. *Fitness Folio.* Published by Lawrence J. Frankel, Cresham Printing Co., Charleston, W.Va. 1967.

Freeman, Larry, M.D. *Self Fulfillment and Aging.* The American Life Foundation & Study Institute, Watkins Glen, N.Y. 1973.

Glueck, Sheldon and Eleanor. *Delinquents in the Making—Paths to Prevention.* Harper and Row.

Glueck, Sheldon and Eleanor. *Physique and Delinquency.* Harper and Row.

Goldthwait, Joel E., M.D. *Body Mechanics in Health and Disease.* J. B. Lippincott Company.

Gourlay, Jack, *Life After 65.* The Associated Press, 1974.

Halberston, Michael, M.D. *The Pills in Your Life.* Grosset and Dunlap, N.Y.

Harris, Raymond, M.D. *The Management of Geriatric Cardiovascular* Disease. J. B. Lippincott Company.

Hawley, Gertrude, M. A. *The Kinesiology of Corrective Exercise.* Lea and Febiger, 1937.

"Health and Fitness in the Modern World." A collection of papers presented at the Institute of Normal Human Anatomy. Published by the Athletic Institute in co-operation with The American College of Sports Medicine.

Heckel, Dr. Francis. *Cultural Physique.* Masson and Co. 1913.

Heinz, H. J. Company. *Nutritional Data.*

Hellman, Lillian, *Pentimento.* Little, Brown and Company, Boston, Toronto, 1973.

Hern, K. M. *Physical Treatment of Injuries of the Brain and Allied Nervous Disorders.* The Williams and Wilkins Co.

Hettinger, Theodor, M.D. *Physiology of Strength.* Charles C. Thomas, 1961.

Hrachovec, Joseph P., M.D., D. Sc., *How To Stay Active & Healthy Past 100.* Sherbourne Press, Los Angeles, Ca. 1972.

Interdisciplinary Topics in Gerontology, Vol. 5. Gitman, L. and Woodford, E. Williams. *Research, Training and Practice in Clinical Medicine of Aging.* S. Karger, Basel, Switzerland, 1970.

"Interdisciplinary Topics in Gerontology, Vol. 1." Chown, Sheila and Riegel, K. F. *Psychological Functioning in the Normal Aging and Senile Aged.* S. Karger, Basel, Switzerland, 1968.

"Interdisciplinary Topics in Gerontology, Vol. 3." Lothenthal, Marjorie Fiske and Zilli, Ario. *Colloquium on Health and Aging of the Population.* S. Karger, Basel, Switzerland, 1969.

"Interdisciplinary Topics in Gerontology, Vol 2." Shanas, Ethel and Madge. J. *Methodological Problems in Cross-National Studies in Aging.* S. Karger, Basel, Switzerland, 1968.

"Interdisciplinary Topics in Gerontology, Vol. 4." Welford, A. T. and Birren, James. *Decision Making and Age.* S. Karger, Basel, Switzerland, 1969.

Jacobson, Edmund, M.D. *Progressive Relaxation.* The University of Chicago Press.

Johnson, Warren. *Science and Medicine of Exercise and Sports.* Harper and Brothers, N.Y. 1960.

Joslin, Elliott P., M.D. Sc. D. *Diabetic Manual.* Lea and Febiger, Publishers.

Jokl, Ernst, M.D. *Research in Physical Education.* University Park Press, 1960.

Jokl, Ernst and McClellan, J. T. *Exercise and Cardiac Death.* University Park Press.

Jokl, E., M.D. *Liggaamsoe Feninge-Physical Exercise*. J. L. Van Schaik, Bpk—Ltd. 1940. Pretoria.

Jokl, E., M.D. *Medicine and Sport*. University of Kentucky 1960. University Park Press.

Jokl, E. and Jokl, P. *Exercise and Altitude*. S. Karger, Basel, Switzerland, 1968.

Jokl, E., M.D. *The Clinical Physiology of Physical Fitness and Rehabilitation*.

Jokl, E., M.D. *Medical Sociology and Cultural Anthropology of Sport and Physical Education*. Charles C. Thomas, Publisher.

Jokl, E., M.D. *The Scope of Exercise in Rehabilitation*. Charles C. Thomas.

Jokl E., M.D. *What Is Sports Medicine?* Charles C. Thomas.

Jokl, E., M.D. *Physiology of Exercise*. Charles C. Thomas.

Jokl, E., M.D. *Nutrition Exercise Body Composition*.

Jokl, E., M.D. *Heart and Sport*. Charles C. Thomas.

Jowett, M. A. *The Dialogues of Plato*. Bigelow, Brown and Company, Inc. N.Y.

Karvonen, M. J. et. al. "Sports in the Cultural Pattern of the World." Institute of Occupational Health, Helsinki, Finalnd.

Karvonen, Martti J., M.D., Ph.D. and Barry, Allan J., Ph.D. *Physical Activity and the Heart*. Charles C. Thomas.

Klafs and Arnheim. *Modern Principles of Athletic Training*. The C. V. Mosby Company.

Knudson, K. A., F. Braae Hansen. *A Text-Book of Gymnastics*. P. Blakiston's Son & Company, Inc. 1937.

Kordel, Lelord. *Eat and Grow Younger*. The World Publishing Company 1952.

Kraus, Hans, M.D. *Backache, Stress and Tension*. Simon and Schuster, 1965.

Kraus, Hans, M.D. *Clinical Treatment of Back and Neck Pain*. McGraw-Hill Book Co., 1970.

Kraus, Hans, M.D. *Therapeutic Exercises*. Charles C. Thomas, 1956.

Kraus, Hans and Wilhelm Raab. *Hypokinetic Disease*. Charles C. Thomas, 1961.

Lamb, Lawrence E., M.D. *Your Heart and How to Live With It*. The Viking Press, Inc. 1969.

Leaf, Alexander, M.D. "Threescore and Forty" *Intellectual Digest*, March 1974.

Licht, Sidney, M.D. *Therapeutic Exercise*. Elizabeth Licht, Publisher, 1961.

Lockhart, R. D., M.D., Ch. M., F.R.S.E. *Anatomy of the Human Body*. J. B. Lippincott Company.

Lowman, Charles LeRoy, M.D., Sc. D., F.A.C.S. and Young, Carl Haven, Ed. C., C. C. T., F.A.A.P.M.R. *Postural Fitness.* Lea and Febiger, 1963.

Loy, John W., Jr. and Kenyon, Gerald S. *Sport, Culture and Society.* The Macmillian Limited, London.

Mandell, Richard D. *The Nazi Olympics.* Macmillan Co. N.Y.

Marchant, E. C. Xenophon—*Memorabilia and Deconomicus.* Harvard University Press.

Maugham, W. Somerset. *The Summing Up.* International Collectors Library American Headquarters, Garden City, N.Y. 1938.

Mayer, Jean, Ph. D. *Overweight.* Prentice-Hall, Inc. 1968.

McGrady, Patrick M. *The Youth Doctors.* Doward-McCann, Inc. N.Y. 1968.

McCurdy, A. M., M.D., M.P.E. *The Physiology of Exercise.* Lea and Febiger.

Menninger, Karl. *Man Against Himself.* Harvest Books.

Mensendieck, Bess M. *The Mensendiech System of Functional Exercises.* The Southworth-Antholnsen Press, 1937, Portland, Me.

Metheny, Eleanor, Ph. D. *Body Dynamics.* McGraw-Hill, 1952.

Miller, Benjamin F., M.D. and Galton, Lawrence. *Freedom From Heart Attacks. Simon and Schuster, 1972.*

Montagu, Ashley. *Touching.* Columbia University Press, 1971.

Morehouse and Miller. *Physiology of Exercise.* The C. V. Mosby Company, 1963.

Morrison, Lester M., M.D. *The Low-Fat Way to Health and Longer Life.* Prentice-Hall, Inc. 1958.

Needles, Robert J., M.D., F.A.C.P. *Your Heart and Common Sense.* Frederick Fell, Inc., N.Y.

Olson, Herbert W., M. A., Michigan State University Index and Abstracts of Foreign Physical Education Literature. Published by Phi Epsilon Kappa Fraternity, Indianapolis, Ind. 1965.

Peale, Robert C., M.D., *Live Longer & Better.* Prentic-Hall, 1961.

Phelps, Winthrop Morgan, B.S., M.D., M.A., F.A.C.S. *The Diagnosis and Treatment of Postural Defects.* Charles Thomas, 1932.

"Physical Education in School." Research Committee of the International Council of Sport and Physical Education at UNESCO, Warsaw, 1962.

Poortmans, J. R. *Biochemistry of Exercise.* University Park Press, Baltimore, Md., 1968.

Prinzmetal, Myron, M.D. and Winter, William, *Patient. Heart Attack: New Hope, New Knowledge, New Life.* Simon and Schuster.

Proceedings of the International Symposium on Physical Activity and Cardiovascular Health. L'Association Me'Dicale Canadienne. Vol. 96, #12, March 25, 1967.

Raab, Wilhelm, M.D. *Prevention of Ischemic Heart Disease.* Charles C. Thomas.

Rabinowitz, Dorothy and Nielsen, Yedida. *Home Life.* The Macmillan Company.

Rodahl, Kaare, M.D. and Horvath, Steven M., Ph.D. *Muscle as a Tissue.* McGraw-Hill Book Co., Inc.

Rasch, Philip J., Ph.D., C.C.T., F.A.C.S.M. and Burke, Roger K., Ph.D., F.A.C.S.M. *Kinesiology and Applied Anatomy.* Lea and Febiger, 1959.

Ricci, Benjamin. *Physiological Basis of Human Performance.* Lea and Febiger, 1967.

Rice, Emmett A. *A Brief History of Physical Education.* The Ronald Press Company, 1958.

Rushmer, Robert F., M.D. *Cardiovascular Dynamics.* W. B. Saunders Company, 1961.

Rodah, Kaare, M.D. *Be Fit For Life.* Harper and Row.

Rosenbaum, Francis F., M.D. and Belknap, Elston L., M.D. *Work and the Heart.* Paul Hoeber, Inc. (Harper & Bros.)

Rusk, Howard. *Living with a Disability.* The Blakiston Co. 1953.

Schneider, Edward C., M.P.E., Ph.D., D. Sc. *Physiology of Muscular Activity.* W. B. Saunders Company, 1940.

Selye, Hans, M.D. *The Stress of Life.* McGraw-Hill Book Co.

Sheldon, William H., Ph.D., M.D. *The Varieties of Temperment.* Harper and Brothers Publishers, 1942.

Sheldon, William H., Ph.D., M.D. *Atlas of Men.* Harper Brothers.

Sheldon, William H., Ph.D., M.D. *The Varieties of Delinquent Youth.* Harper Brothers.

Sheldon, William H., Ph. D., M.D. *The Varieties of Human Physique.* Harper and Brothers Publishers. 1940.

Simenon, Georges, *When I was Old.* A Helen and Kurt Wolff Book. Harcourt Brace Jovanovich, Inc., 757 Third Ave., N.Y., N.Y. 10017, 1970.

Simon, E. and Jokl, E. *International Research in Sport and Physical Education.* Charles C. Thomas, 1964.

Simonson, Ernest (Conference) *Measurement in Exercise Electrocardiography.* Charles C. Thomas.

Smith, Bert Kruger. *Aging in America.* Beacon Press, Boston, Mass. 1973.

Smout, C.F.V., M.D., M.R.C.S., L.R.C.P. and McDowall, R.J.S. *Anatomy and Physiology.* The Williams and Wilkins Company.

Spencer, Herbert. *The Principles of Sociology.* D. Appleton and Company, 1898.

Smith, Olive F. Guthrie, M.B.E. C.S.P., Y.M.G. *Rehabilitation, Re-Education and Remedial Exercises.* Williams and Wilkins Company.

Stern, Frances. *Applied Dietetics.* Williams and Wilkins Co. 1943.

Strecker, Edward A., A.M., M.D. and Ebaugh, Franklin G., A.S., M.D. *Practical Clinical Psychiatry.* P. Blakiston's Son and Company, Inc.

Steindler, Arthur, M.D., F.A.C.S. *Mechanics of Normal and Pathological Locomotion in Man.*

Sumption, Dorothy. *Fundamental Danish Gymnastics for Women.* A. S. Barnes and Company, 1932.

Taylor, Gordon Raitray. *The Biological Time Bomb.* The World Publishing Co.

Taylor, Robert B. *Feeling Alive After 65,* Arlington House Publishers, 81 Centre Ave., New Rochelle, N.Y. 10801, 1973.

Thompson, Clem W., Ph.D., F.A.C.S.M. *Kranz-Manual of Kinesiology.* The C. V. Mosby Company, 1961.

Thulin, J. G. *Gymnastikatlas.* Publisher: Svenska Gymnastik Forbundets Bokserie.

Townsend, Claire. *Old Age: The Last Segregation.* Bantam Books Inc., 666 Fifth Ave., N.Y., N.Y. 10019, 1971.

Supt. of Documents, United States Senate Special Committee on Aging, August 25, 1969. Part 7—International Perspectives, Washington, D.C. United States Gov't. Printing Office, Washington, 1970.

Vesey, G.N.A. *Body and Mind.* London, George Allen and Unwin, Ltd.

Wartenweiler, Zurich. Biomechanics. S. Karger, Basel, Switzerland, 1963.

Wells, Harry K. & Ivan P. Pavlov. *Toward a Scientific Psychology and Psychiatry.* International Publishers, N.Y. 1956.

Westmann, Stephan K. *Sport, Physical Training and Womanhood.* The Williams and Wilkins Company, 1939.

Westermarck, Edward. *The History of Human Marriage.* The Allerton Book Company.

White, Paul Dudly, M.D. *My Life and Medicine.* Gambit, Inc. 1971.

Williams, Jesse Feiring, M.D., Sc. D. *A Textbook of Anatomy and Physiology.*

Williams, Marian, and Worthington, Catherine. *Therapeutic Exercise for Body Alignment and Function.* W. B. Saunders Co.

Winter, Ruth. *Ageless Aging.* Crown Publishers, Inc., New York, 1973.